The
Logistics
of Literacy
Intervention

A PLANNING GUIDE FOR MIDDLE AND HIGH SCHOOLS

by Joanne Klepeis Allain, MA

Sopris West™
EDUCATIONAL SERVICES

A Cambium Learning Company

BOSTON, MA · LONGMONT, CO

Printed in the United States of America
Published and Distributed by

Sopris West™
EDUCATIONAL SERVICES

A Cambium Learning Company

4093 Specialty Place • Longmont, Colorado 80504
(303) 651-2829 • www.sopriswest.com

152645/310/03-07

ABOUT THE AUTHOR

Joanne Klepeis Allain received her master's degree in secondary curriculum and instruction from California State Polytechnic University in 1998. Her tenure in education has focused on at-risk youth, specifically adolescents who struggle to read. Joanne served for many years at both the classroom and district levels for the Los Angeles County Office of Education, Alternative Education Programs, whose target population includes students expelled from school. The literacy challenges presented by Joanne's students led to her interest and study in the field of adolescent literacy.

Joanne has served as a graduate-level instructor for California State Polytechnic University and the University of California–Los Angeles. She is a national trainer for *LANGUAGE!® The Comprehensive Literacy Curriculum* and was named Trainer of the Year in 2005. Joanne has presented at national and international conferences that focus on the needs of at-risk youth and the educational systems that serve them.

Joanne is currently in private practice as a literacy consultant, focusing on implementation of literacy intervention for districts across the country. She resides in Long Beach, Calif., with her husband, Jim Cloonan, and two Redbone hounds, Leon and Lizzie.

To inquire about literacy intervention planning at your school or district, e-mail Joanne at toimagn@ix.netcom.com.

DEDICATION

To my family, friends, and colleagues who encouraged and nudged me along the way. I am forever grateful. Special thanks to my parents, Frank and Catherine; my husband, Jim; and my children, Brian and Jeanie, who are always my inspiration.

> We have to teach the children we have;
> Not the children we used to have,
> Not the children we want to have,
> Not the children we dream to have.
>
> —*Woodrow Wilson*

CONTENTS

Introduction

As an educational consultant focusing on the implementation of literacy intervention, it heartens me to see the efforts that districts and schools across the country are making to address the needs of older struggling readers. I have had the opportunity to observe and study the implementation of intervention in school districts over a period of years, and I have seen the ebb and flow of progress and challenge. In every case, good intentions, excellent materials, and willing teachers have not been enough to sustain meaningful intervention without a comprehensive long-range implementation plan. Schools that have invested the time and energy to formulate and institutionalize plans have garnered success. Those with superficial plans—but good intentions—made valiant starts, but watched enthusiasm recede with every challenge as the status quo returned. Students ultimately revert to disengaged recipients of an educational process in which they cannot fully participate, and the achievement gap widens.

A vast number of middle school and high school students are reading significantly below grade-level. The Nation's Report Card, 2005 (Perie, Grigg, & Donahue, 2005), reports that 27 percent of eighth graders are reading below basic levels, and only 31 percent of eighth-grade students are performing at levels considered proficient or above. Dropout rates for high school students are staggering; we are losing 29 percent prior to graduation. Minority numbers increase dramatically, with 44 percent of African American students and 48 percent of Hispanic students failing to graduate (Greene & Winters, 2005). There are many conjectures as to why students fail to graduate. Jeanne Chall (2000, p. 123) aptly describes what is certainly one of the primary causes: "It is quite reasonable to expect students to drop out when they know they are failing. It is painful to keep exposing oneself to continued failure. And it must be deeply humiliating to a high school student to have the teacher read the textbook to the class because they are not able to read it themselves—or to have the teacher rewrite parts of the textbook so that it can be read by the students. Why, they may ask, did no one in the school take them aside and teach them to read and write long before they got to high school? Or send them to a school that could do it?"

In response to the adolescent literacy crisis, local, state, and national educational institutions are allocating more resources to reading intervention. The recognition that our adolescent readers require help cannot come fast enough (Underwood & Pearson, 2004). Unfortunately, funding alone will not answer the many questions that challenge districts as they attempt to meet the needs of their middle school and high school struggling readers. What type of intervention is the most effective? How do we meet grade-level requirements and still teach literacy? Who will teach this? How do we implement a plan? What does literacy intervention look like at the middle school and high school levels? How do we know if intervention is working?

One of the first challenges for middle school and high school administration is to determine the type of literacy instruction necessary for their struggling readers. The components necessary to teach early reading have been clearly outlined in current reading research. The report of the National Reading Panel (National Institute of Child Health and Human Development [NICHD], 2000) defined five essential components to effectively teach reading: phonemic awareness, phonics, fluency, vocabulary, and comprehension strategies. In addition to these five skills, writing, speaking, and listening are crucial criteria for success in middle school and high school (Kamil, 2003). However, the developmental needs of the adolescent are not as clear. Middle school and high school students do not come to us as blank slates; they have learned pieces and parts of the reading process as they have struggled through school, and we must address their specific needs (Moats, 2001).

Although there is some divergence as to the emphasis for each of the five skills at the middle school and high school levels, there is general agreement that older struggling students must demonstrate proficiency in all prerequisite skills outlined by the National Reading Panel (NICHD, 2000) if we expect them to comprehend and interact with grade-level text (Biancarosa & Snow, 2004; Kamil, 2003; Moats, 2001; Pressley, 2001). Perhaps the most disputed skill is decoding—the ability to sound out words. It is estimated that as many as one in ten adolescents struggles to identify words (Curtis, 2004). The research estimates that 8.7 million grade 4–12 students struggle to read, which translates into 870,000 students who lack basic decoding skills (Kamil, 2003). According to Curtis (2004, p. 122), "Such readers can end up engaging more in composing what they read than in comprehending what has been written." The message of the research is clear: we cannot discount any of the skills necessary for literacy just because students are older. We must carefully assess our students to determine which skills are needed and which skills deserve the most emphasis. We must then provide comprehensive instruction in all areas of need (Kamil, 2003).

The duration and methodology needed to teach effective literacy intervention is less controversial. Researchers agree that students struggling to read require explicit (nothing is random or left to chance) and systematic instruction in literacy skills as well as ample opportunities for practice and application in authentic text (Biancarosa & Snow, 2004; Kamil, 2003; Lyon, 2006; Moats, 2001; Torgensen, 2004). Explicit, or direct, instruction is a major instructional shift for middle school and high school teachers.

Struggling adolescent readers can be loosely divided into two groups; descriptive terms for these groups vary by state or researcher. According to the Reading/Language Arts Framework for California Public Schools (Kame'enui & Simmons, 1999, pp. 227–228), struggling students are identified as either *strategic* or *intensive*. *Strategic students* are described as "one to two deviations below the mean according to the results of standardized testing." *Intensive students* are described as "seriously at risk as indicated by their extremely and chronically low performance on one or more measures." The practical considerations for literacy instruction for both strategic and intensive learners are time, intensity, and content of literacy instruction. Luckily, current research has provided the necessary content, and many publishers have developed tools specifically designed to address struggling middle school and high school readers.

Beyond developing comprehensive instructional plans for strategic and intensive learners, schools are faced with the daunting task of implementing literacy-based school reform. Biancarosa and Snow (2004, p. 13) write: "While the instructional improvements can have tremendous impact, it is important to realize that they would be more effective if they were implemented in conjunction with infrastructural supports. Furthermore, the instructional improvements are unlikely to be maintained or extended beyond the original intervention classrooms if these infrastructural factors are not in place." Even the best intentions, instructional materials, and strategies will not result in significant student progress if we do not develop practical plans to ensure that teachers can do the job we expect of them.

So we come to the purpose of *The Logistics of Literacy Intervention*. As part of my consulting services, I began developing logistical steps in response to specific intervention agendas of educators. I created plans and worksheets based on successful school plans with significant student progress, and I outlined steps that were missed along the way. The work progressed into a handbook—this book—for educators to initiate, implement, and sustain quality literacy intervention. I developed this book with the intention of disassembling the big idea of middle school and high school literacy reform and of assisting school districts in designing practical, effective implementation plans. This book is not a guide for choosing specific reading intervention programs, but rather a series of steps, worksheets, and checklists that will enable educators to think about the everyday implications of literacy intervention.

The organization of *The Logistics of Literacy Intervention* follows the three phases of school reform developed by Michael Fullan (2001):

+ **Initiation**—The process that results in the decision to move forward with a literacy intervention initiative.
+ **Implementation**—The process of putting literacy intervention into practice, which can span one to three years.
+ **Continuance**—The processes that result in the institutionalization of literacy intervention that can withstand changes in funding, configuration, and personnel change. Continuance is informed by both reading and school-reform researchers in order to provide a more complete picture of literacy intervention at the district and school levels.

In addition, I have added a conclusive wrap-up:

+ **Parting Words**—The process of articulating and codifying details of the literacy implementation plan in order to provide coherence for all stakeholders as literacy intervention progresses from initiation to implementation to continuance.

So, let the planning begin. Our struggling students are waiting for us!

Initiation

PHASE 1: *Initiation*

Fullan (2001) describes the process of initiation as the period in which an innovation or improvement project is adopted or a decision is made to move forward. Applied to literacy intervention, initiation begins the moment that the district or the school acknowledges the need to address their struggling readers. The initiation phase sets the stage for the quality of implementation and sustainability of literacy intervention at the district and school site. During this phase, educators develop a set of ideals, goals, and policies that will promote unity of purpose around what students should learn, how they should learn it, and how the school and personnel must be organized to meet the needs of struggling readers (Hill & Celio, 1998).

Once the need for intervention is acknowledged, a series of events occur that will develop into the district and school literacy intervention plan. Decisions that need to be made during this period include: (1) how many students need intervention; (2) how many students can be served based on fiscal, physical, and human resources; and (3) how the inclusion of literacy intervention will affect the school system. The students are identified, the number is calculated, and the investigation begins as to what type of intervention is needed for both strategic and intensive students based on current reading research as well as the practical implications of site implementation.

The following sections provide guidance for the district or school that is ready to initiate literacy intervention by asking hard questions and developing a systematic, concrete plan.

Setting Priorities

THE CHALLENGE

Millions of middle school and high school students do not read at proficient levels. Increased awareness and accountability regarding student failure put districts in an extreme catch-up mode as they try to address the needs of their struggling readers. The market is flooded with versions of the latest, greatest "fix" for reading failure, and each claims to be research-based. District administrators are faced with a plethora of choices as well as implementing structures that are new to middle schools and high schools. However, districts often fail to weigh innovations relative to the impact they will have on basic educational goals and priorities (Fullan, 2001). Without setting priorities, literacy intervention may be viewed as merely one more reform initiative in a sea of projects that promises to make a difference in students' lives; thus, literacy intervention does not receive the attention it needs.

THE SOLUTION

It is the primary goal of the educational system to produce students who are literate and able to participate in a democratic society. The hard question is: What are we willing to do to achieve that goal? The decision to move ahead with literacy intervention involves more than purchasing materials and training teachers. At the middle school and high school levels, the systems and structures must also change to address the needs of the students who struggle. Middle schools and high schools must evolve from content-centered to student-centered institutions. Districts and schools must assess the importance of literacy relative to other pressing goals. Intervention will work only if it is a priority goal. It is, therefore, crucial that the district or school recognize the importance of literacy intervention and measure its value against other pressing needs. That is not to say that other school-improvement projects should be discarded; rather, projects should be analyzed based on the impact each will have on the school's primary goals (Fullan, 2001). We must remember that innovations such as literacy intervention are designed to serve students, not school structure. Keeping the welfare of students in mind helps to prioritize innovations. Ask yourself: What happens to students if we don't adopt literacy intervention?

> *"Middle schools and high schools must evolve from content-centered to student-centered institutions ... (Literacy) intervention will work only if it is a priority goal rather than an 'add-on' program."*

KEYS TO SUCCESS

Questions to consider:

- What percentage of students will benefit from reading intervention?
- Will effective reading intervention result in higher student achievement in all content areas?
- Is the district willing to make literacy intervention a priority for at least five to eight years?
- Will literacy intervention reduce the dropout rate?
- Will the district/school dedicate resources to ensure that the literacy intervention is implemented for the term of the plan and beyond, if necessary?
- What are the social and emotional benefits of assisting struggling readers?
- How will reading intervention affect federal and state accountability measures?
- How will reading intervention affect the school culture?
- Will literacy intervention make a difference in students' lives after high school?

THE WORKSHEET

Use Worksheet 1.1 to itemize current and pending improvement projects and to analyze their relative importance to student achievement:

- List projects and analyze their potential effect(s) on district or school goals as they relate to student achievement and each other.
- Rate the projects on a scale from 1–5 (5 being highest) to prioritize and consider the academic benefit of each project.
- This activity serves as a catalyst for a discussion about priority levels and specific resources that reading intervention will receive if planned and implemented.

Worksheet 1.1 *Setting Priorities*

Improvement Project	Improves student performance in all content areas and/or subjects	Helps students meet state and federal standards	Raises standardized test scores	Assists school to meet AYP goals	Raises student self-esteem	Helps close the achievement gap	Improves graduation rates	Progress can be measured

The Literacy Intervention Coordinator and the District Literacy Intervention Committee

THE CHALLENGE

District and school administrators are already overwhelmed with improvement projects, account-ability measures, students, parents, and teachers. The capacity of district support staff is stretched thin, and administrators must wear many hats. However, implementing literacy intervention is a monumental task that requires and deserves the full attention of the person in charge. Forming a group with expertise in systematic instruction and the workings of middle school and high school is, in itself, a challenging task. The Literacy Intervention Coordinator and District Literacy Intervention Committee must not only plan and support a large-scale systemic reform but also must be willing to listen to and consider all sides of an issue. The coordinator and committee members must be strong enough to withstand resistance and understanding enough to appreciate that the implementers will need nurturing, respect, and support during the process.

THE SOLUTION

The goal of selecting a Literacy Intervention Coordinator and District Literacy Intervention Committee is to provide effective leadership in improving the literacy skills of struggling students. The committee guides and directs instructional improvement at the district level (Elmore, 2000). Certainly, in a per-fect world, the coordinator and committee members would step forward voluntarily. In the absence of volunteers, however, it is wise to choose a coordinator and committee members who either have expertise in research-based literacy instruction or are willing to embrace the academic con-tent and pedagogy.

"The committee should represent all stakeholders who will be affected by the literacy intervention effort, including district administrators, site administrators, teachers, parents, and union representatives."

The committee should represent all stakeholders who will be affected by the literacy interven-tion effort, including district administrators, site administrators, teachers, parents, and union representatives. Equally important is the inclusion of representatives of various student popula-tions, such as general education, special education, and English language learners (ELLs). It is wise to choose individuals who possess the commitment and passion needed to help struggling readers from a research perspective that embodies high expectations rather than a feel-good philosophy.

Organizational and communication skills are essential. The committee candidates must understand the inherent challenges in teaching reading at the middle school and high school levels. Look for leaders who embody enthusiasm and hope. Their passion is contagious, and others will be infused with their energy (Fullan, 2003). They believe that it is not only the right of all students to be literate, it is also the responsibility of the educational institution to ensure the acquisition of these skills.

KEYS TO SUCCESS

1. Seek out a Literacy Intervention Coordinator and District Literacy Intervention Committee members who:
   - Believe that all students want to, can, and deserve to be literate.
   - Exhibit expertise in middle and high school systems.
   - Are process-aware but product-oriented.
   - Demonstrate respect for, and elicit respect from, all members of the educational community.
   - Are willing to bridge the territorialism that may exist among departments for the good of all students.
   - Possess knowledge and/or are willing to research, learn, and embrace current literacy research as it applies to intervention.
   - Are familiar with assessment instruments and data analysis as they pertain to literacy.
   - Demonstrate the ability to think of what could be rather than what is.
   - Are effective communicators.
   - Demonstrate excellent organizational skills.
2. Articulate District Literacy Intervention Committee tasks, including but not limited to:
   - Develop a literacy mission statement and goals.
   - Determine the level(s) of student need.
   - Determine and secure funding for long-term implementation.
   - Review and recommend instructional materials and strategies.
   - Develop a comprehensive 5–8 year plan.
   - Develop accountability and support criteria for implementers.
   - Monitor student, teacher, and administrator progress at regular intervals.
   - Present progress reports before the school board.
   - Organize and present awareness sessions.
   - Organize initial training.
   - Choose data-screening and progress-monitoring instruments.
   - Help to reorganize school schedules.
3. Prepare sample interview questions for potential intervention teachers, such as:
   - Why is literacy intervention important for middle school and high school students?
   - What are the necessary components of literacy intervention for middle school and high school students?
   - What qualities do you believe are necessary to be an effective literacy-intervention teacher?

- If student scores are not showing progress, what steps would you take to identify the problem(s)?
- The school board wants to know how students will access local and state grade-level standards if they are enrolled in literacy intervention. How would you respond?
- A parent wants an explanation of why his/her child is being placed in an intervention class. How would you respond?
- The District Literacy Intervention Committee members disagree about the type of instruction necessary for literacy intervention. What would you do?
- An administrator is openly opposed to literacy intervention and does not support the district mandate at his/her school. What steps do you believe should be taken?

THE WORKSHEETS

Worksheets 1.2a and 1.2b are simply guides to help you begin to assess the qualifications and qualities of a Literacy Intervention Coordinator and District Literacy Intervention Committee candidates. Grade each candidate from 1–5 (5 being highest) under each category. The worksheets are merely starting points; they are not meant to be all-encompassing documents. Remember that good interview skills don't guarantee good performance. Always check candidates' credentials and references, and talk to their coworkers, supervisors, and subordinates.

Phase 1

Worksheet 1.2a *The Literacy Intervention Coordinator candidates*

Name of Candidate	Expertise in current reading research	Organizational skills	Communication skills	Knowledge of secondary systems	Additional comments or qualifications

Worksheet 1.2b *The District Literacy Intervention Committee candidates*

Name of Candidate	Area of expertise and current position	Secondary Experience (Yes/No)	Organizational skills	Familiar with reading research	Communication skills	Familiar with assessment tools for reading	Additional comments or qualifications

Phase 1

Section 1.3

Mission Statement and Goals

THE CHALLENGE

Most school districts develop a comprehensive mission statement that describes the ideals of the educational institution. Phrases such as "create lifelong learners" or "prepare students to compete in a global society" are usually embedded in the statement. The District Literacy Intervention Committee is charged with establishing a literacy mission statement and a set of goals that will realize the district's vision. All implementers must be able to embrace the mission and goals developed by the committee to ensure the success of literacy intervention. The mission statement and goals will drive the district/school literacy implementation. Articulation of the objectives will set the stage for the success or failure of intervention; the committee must have a clear idea of what is necessary and what is attainable. The major stumbling block at this point is that the implementers (i.e., the site administrators and teachers) may view the literacy effort as a superficial stab at doing the right thing. The committee must create a mission statement and goals that are clear and focused and avoid the illusion of what Fullan (2001, p. 77) describes as "false clarity": "False clarity occurs when the change is interpreted in an oversimplified way; that is, the proposed change has more to it than people perceive or realize." Without a clear mission statement and goals, implementers may not realize that literacy intervention will affect their entire school system—including teaching practice—and thus not give the intervention effort the dedication and attention it deserves. However, the mission and goals cannot be so complex or overwhelming that implementers see them as unattainable.

THE SOLUTION

Instructional improvement is based on the idea that everyone clearly understands the magnitude of the change and values the significance of its effect on student achievement. If literacy intervention is to succeed, everyone must be on the same page; Elmore (2000) describes this as "organizational coherence." The mission and goals of the committee must be rigorous yet reasonable; the mission is a statement of intent as to what the district/school will do to ensure that the district vision is realized through literacy intervention, and the goals are benchmarks against which progress is measured.

In *Raising Reading Achievement in Middle and High Schools*, Elaine K. McEwan (2001, p. 11) provides the example of Lincoln School, whose solely stated and measurable goal was to "reduce the number of students performing in the bottom quartile by 10 percent." Clearly, this is a goal that all could embrace. Individual school goals may go even further by quantifying the percentage (e.g., 50 fewer students will perform below the 20th percentile at the end of the first year of literacy intervention). Of course, the actual number is relative to the number of students receiving intervention. The challenge for the District

Literacy Intervention Committee, then, is to set goals that can be enacted by all stakeholders, measured for progress, and revisited yearly for revision. Hill and Celio (1998, p. 32) do an excellent job of explaining the importance of developing clear goals: "Schools that expect to make a major difference in what children know and can do have very clear goals, and they have definite methods of pursuing these goals. The goals and methods color every transaction among faculty members and between faculty, students, parents, and other constituencies."

"The challenge for the District Literacy Intervention Committee, then, is to set goals that can be enacted by all stakeholders, measured for progress, and revisited yearly for revision."

Goal-setting is not for students alone. In addition to student progress goals, the District Literacy Intervention Committee should set measurable goals for themselves. In order to measure the success of the literacy intervention effort, everyone must be held accountable. Therefore, the committee must articulate group performance goals for the first and subsequent years, and then review and revise those goals as needed.

KEYS TO SUCCESS

- Be reasonable. Choose a mission statement and goals that are ambitious, yet realistic.
- Use specific language. Educational jargon may not be clear to students and parents.
- Develop a process to revisit and revise goals each year based on student and teacher progress.
- Develop a mission statement and goals that are measurable and can be supported by funds, personnel, and materials.
- Talk to administrators and teachers about their vision of a fully literate student body prior to beginning the discussion.
- If necessary, consult a professional to facilitate the process and keep the group on-task.

THE WORKSHEETS

Use Worksheet 1.3a to help you review the current district/school vision and develop a literacy mission statement. Sample mission statement:

> It is the mission of the Northern District to provide quality intervention to all middle school and high school students who struggle to read and write. General education students, special education students, and English language learners are identified and provided with instruction to meet their assessed needs. As a result of literacy instruction taught with fidelity, students will make measurable progress toward performing at grade-level.

Use Worksheets 1.3b–1.3e to help you develop goals for student progress and for the District Literacy Intervention Committee.

Worksheet 1.3a *District/School Vision and Literacy Mission Statement*

1. Write the current District/School Vision in the space below.

2. Use the current District/School Vision to develop a Literacy Mission Statement. Make the Statement short and to the point.

Worksheet 1.3b *Student Progress Goals*

(sample)

Goal	Measurement	Achieved (Yes/No)	Response actions
Year 1 – Sample			
5% fewer students will perform below the 20th percentile on standardized assessments.			
Literacy intervention students will show improvement on progress-monitoring assessment tools.			
Behavior referrals for literacy intervention students will decrease by 5%.			
Attendance of literacy intervention will improve.			
Year 1			
Year 2			

Phase 1

Worksheet 1.3c *Student Progress Goals*

Goal	Measurement	Achieved (Yes/No)	Response actions
Year 1			
Year 2			
Year 3			

Worksheet 1.3d *Literacy Committee Goals (Year 1)*

(sample)

Sample goals	Lead person	Due date	Notes
1. Develop a vision, mission, and student progress goals.			
2. Identify and administer a screening and diagnostic instrument to assess student need and placement.			
3. Train teachers to administer and evaluate screening and diagnostic assessments.			
4. Identify and validate research-based curricula for strategic and intensive students in grades 6–12.			
5. Provide awareness sessions for administrators, teachers, counselors, and parents.			
6. Draft and present a literacy intervention resolution for adoption by the board of education.			
7. Draft a proposal in the performance plan of administrators and teachers to include progress of literacy intervention students.			
8. Select and train teachers and administrators.			
9. Develop a template for schools to develop a school-site implementation plan.			
10. Order and distribute materials to school sites.			
11. Provide follow-up training for teachers and administrators throughout the year.			

Phase 1

Worksheet 1.3e *Literacy Committee Goals (Year 1)*

Sample goals	Lead person	Due date	Notes

Funding

THE CHALLENGE

Certainly in a time of budget reductions, identifying funds that can be dedicated to a long-term reform effort is a significant challenge. Each department within a district depends on funding to support the goals of their respective populations. There are too many needs and so little money. Since funding amounts and sources may change from year to year, finding monies that can be dedicated to an intervention effort over many years is tenuous, at best. The temptation is to look at literacy intervention as a short-term effort: provide intervention for one or two years, hope that a miracle will occur, and all students will be performing at grade-level. While this type of wishful thinking is appealing, it is unrealistic. Literacy intervention is a long-term improvement project and thus requires funding that can support and sustain it.

THE SOLUTION

The members of the District Literacy Intervention Committee are chosen for two primary reasons: (1) to bring the expertise of the stakeholders to the table for intervention discussion and planning; and (2) to coordinate intellectual and funding resources for intervention implementation and continuation.

Three major groups of students are candidates for literacy intervention: (1) general education; (2) special education; and (3) ELLs. If students from any of these groups demonstrate a need for intervention, then funding sources that support the population can be used. Literacy intervention is not something that can be started and then discarded when purse strings are tight. Of all the meaningful things we do for our students, teaching them to read and write is not an optional exercise. It is our primary objective, since all academic success depends on students' ability to negotiate grade-level instruction. When reviewing funding, it is important to identify all possible sources and determine what aspects of intervention each source will cover. For example, one funding source may cover instructional materials while another might focus on professional development. Both are needed for literacy intervention. Also, consider blending classes. If a class is made up of general education, special

> *"When reviewing funding, it is important to identify all possible sources and determine what aspects of intervention each source will cover ... If a class is made up of general education, special education, and ELL students, then funding from all three sources can support the (intervention) class."*

education, and ELL students, then funding from all three sources can support the class. Remember that most funding sources—both public and private—require an end goal of student achievement. The purpose of literacy intervention is to increase student achievement and thus supports the criteria of many funding sources.

KEYS TO SUCCESS

- Research both private and public funding sources.
- Work with the parent organization as a possible fundraising source.
- Phone or e-mail local, state, and federal consultants to see which funding sources would support literacy intervention. They will help you negotiate the language of funding requirements.
- All literacy intervention publishers need student achievement data for validation of their curricula. Publishers may be willing to work with the district on materials, training, or assessment.
- Publishers often have information on funding sources for districts that are interested in adopting a particular curriculum and are willing to help.
- Consult the grant writers in your school district to apply for literacy grants.
- Consult the state and federal education agencies for grant opportunities.
- Include all possible funding sources for general education, special education, and ELL students.
- Identify funding sources that can be dedicated to a long-term plan.

THE WORKSHEETS

Use Worksheet 1.4a to assist in collecting information about various funding sources, specific amounts, and the designated criteria for spending. Use Worksheet 1.4b to help you estimate possible costs that will arise as you go through the source-funding process. This worksheet will serve as the initial guideline for allocating funds. Columns are provided to list the sources and amounts of funding that can be designated for each item.

Worksheet 1.4a *Literacy Intervention Funding Streams*

Funding	Fund Type _____	Fund Type _____	Fund Type _____	Fund Type _____	TOTAL _____
Population (total amount available)					
Special education					
English language learners (ELLs)					
General education					
At-risk students					
Free and reduced lunch					
Middle school					
High school					
After-school programs					
Teachers					
Administrators					
Materials (total amount available)					
Teacher materials					
Student materials					
Classroom supplies					
Professional Development (total amount available)					
Training room					
Audiovisual					
Food					
Substitute teachers					
Trainer fee					
Trainer expenses (e.g., airfare, meals, lodging)					
Follow-up training					
Coaches					
Administrator training					
Counselor training					
Data Collection (total amount available)					
Pre- and post-assessment materials					
Assessment administration and training					
Data collection					
Data analysis					
Technology for data collection					
TOTALS					

Phase 1

Worksheet 1.4b *Literacy Intervention Estimated Cost Sheet*

Item	Special education	ELLs	General Education	Total cost	Funds available	Difference
Materials						
Student						
Teacher						
Training						
Administrator						
Supplies						
Training						
Training fees						
Trainer expenses						
Training room						
Audiovisual						
Food						
Substitutes						
Administrator						
Teacher						
Paraprofessional						
Parents						
Follow-up						
Coaches						
Data Collection						
Materials						
Training						
Administration						
Collection						
Analysis						
Technology						
Personnel						

Determining Student Need

THE CHALLENGE

The number of students eligible for literacy intervention—including both intensive and strategic students—will dictate the scope of the implementation plan. When reviewing district mission and funding sources, it is up to the District Literacy Intervention Committee to determine how many students require service. The sheer magnitude of student need can overwhelm district personnel; the district must not only consider funding allocations but also personnel, class schedules, and parent notification. Districts might also encounter political ramifications of identifying large numbers of students who are not meeting grade-level expectations. Dr. Alex Granzin (2006) aptly expresses the immediacy of the issue: "Why don't we just stop everything when kids aren't learning to read? I mean, why are we even doing anything else? When kids don't master this process, why doesn't the red light start flashing immediately and say, 'Wait a minute, we're not moving on.' We're not going to treat this as though it is some sort of small problem that we can solve by sending you over here for a few extra minutes a day and possibly monitoring your progress a little bit more closely and hoping for the best." The need can be staggering. If students do not develop literacy skills by middle school or high school, this is their last chance. It is unlikely that everything else will stop while we address the needs of our struggling readers. So the question that haunts us is: how and where do we start?

THE SOLUTION

A district may decide either to intervene with all students in need of literacy instruction or to grow the intervention. One district may choose to include all students in grades 6–12 performing below the 40th percentile on standardized tests; another district may opt to target only middle-school students who are below the 20th percentile on standardized tests for intensive intervention and then grow the intervention by grade and percentile. The position a district takes will depend on available funding and personnel. It is a difficult decision to make, since all students in need should certainly receive help; however, we must be realistic and effectively address as many students as we can.

"A district may decide either to intervene with all students in need of literacy instruction or to grow the intervention."

Phase 1

KEYS TO SUCCESS

- Identify a qualifying measure for students to receive screening for literacy intervention.
- Use standardized assessments and student grades to determine which students are eligible for literacy intervention.
- Determine which students qualify for strategic or intensive literacy intervention.
- Administer a second screening or curriculum placement measure to determine where a student will place within the intervention band or to determine if students were identified incorrectly. Remember that some students do not test well or may decide to play "connect-the-dots" when they take standardized assessments.
- Choose a diagnostic assessment that provides information on basic literacy skills including, but not limited to, comprehension and fluency.
- Develop a plan for administering the second screening, including collecting and analyzing data.
- Determine the total number of students in need of strategic intervention or intensive intervention.
- Determine the number of classes and teachers needed to serve the students based on the smallest student-teacher ratio possible.
- Utilize a single elective for strategic students.
- Establish a two-period block of instruction for intensive students. This block may include two elective periods or one core period and one elective period (e.g., English 9a and an elective class) to form the intensive literacy class.

THE WORKSHEETS

The series of worksheets that follow will help you document student need and determine the scope of your implementation plan. Use Worksheet 1.5a to assist in identifying initial screening instruments that define student eligibility for intervention. Use Worksheet 1.5b to articulate which additional screening instruments will be used to verify student placement in an intervention class. Use Worksheet 1.5c to provide a structure for identifying and classifying the student population that qualifies for intervention. (Worksheet 1.5c applies the previous worksheets' information to determine the number of students who qualify for intervention.) Worksheet 1.5d functions as a first look at the number of potential classes and teachers that will impact personnel and scheduling decisions.

Worksheet 1.5a *Determining Need (primary sources)*

First screening for literacy intervention: Grades _____ to _____

First screening	Strategic criteria	Intensive criteria	How collected?	Submitted to	Due date
Standardized test					
Content grade average					
Teacher recommendation					
Individual education plan (IEP)					
English proficiency					

Worksheet 1.5b *Determining Need (secondary sources)*

Second screening assessments: Grades _____ to _____

Placement screening assessments	Name of assessment	Qualifying score (Strategic)	Qualifying score (Intensive)	Whole class or individual?	Date of administration	Due date
Fluency						
Word attack						
Comprehension						
Encoding						
Grammar						
Writing sample						

Phase 1

Worksheet 1.5c *Determining Need (quantify number of students)*

Total number of qualifying students in (district/school name) _____

Grade	General education	Special education	ELLs	Strategic	Intensive	TOTALS
6						
7						
8						
9						
10						
11						
12						
TOTALS						

Worksheet 1.5d *Determining Need (quantify number of classes and teachers)*

Numbers of classes and teachers in (school name) _____

Grade	Number of students	Strategic	Intensive	Number of classes ratio _____	Number of teachers	TOTALS
6						
7						
8						
9						
10						
11						
12						
TOTALS						

Choosing Curricula

THE CHALLENGE

Acknowledgment of the need for literacy intervention has swept across the country. Publishers have jumped into the market with various curricula designed to meet student needs. Each curriculum claims to be the silver bullet that will "cure" reading difficulties. Varying philosophies abound, and every curriculum claims to be research-based. Enormous amounts of money are required for materials, and everyone keeps their fingers crossed that intervention will work. Intervention curricula are very different in content and methodology than current middle school and high school instruction. Educators may shun off-the-shelf or packaged curricula and strategies in favor of intervening in their own way. So, how can you know which program is appropriate for intensive and strategic students?

THE SOLUTION

Do your homework and choose carefully. In an article for Educational Leadership, Dr. Louisa C. Moats (2001, p. 39) discusses curricular approaches that have been successful with older struggling readers: "All of these approaches assume that older poor readers can learn to read if they are taught the foundation language skills they missed and if they have ample opportunity to apply the skills in meaning to text reading." She goes on to state: "Beyond third grade, poor readers can be taught if the program has all the necessary components, the teacher is well prepared, and the students are given time, sufficiently intensive instruction, and incentives to overcome their reading and language challenges. Given the right approach, students will buy in. In fact, they'll ask why they were allowed to go so far without being taught to read."

Dr. Edward Kame'enui (2004) states: "You're going to need a curriculum that's very different in architecture for the kids who are in the bottom 20, 25 percent, because the way they manage information is very different from the kids who can benefit from the core. That kind of curriculum we refer to as an intervention curriculum because the architecture is very different. The architecture should be more careful in how it thinks about the examples that are used, how it juxtaposes examples, the amount of scaffolding and teacher-wording that's provided, the amount of practice, how much practice is given at any given point in time, how much scaffolding is provided, how much rehearsal, how much fluency is built in." Moats (2001) and Kame'enui confirm that literacy intervention is a departure from the status quo of instructional content and methodology common to middle school and high school.

Reading science has done much to inform the components necessary for effective intervention. Even though excellent curricula have been developed, some educators are reluctant to consider them. However, if the intervention meets student need, contains the necessary components of

"… a comprehensive plan must be developed for the systemic changes that will occur as the result of literacy intervention. When reviewing curricula, it is also important to consider the skill level of implementing teachers relative to reading instruction."

literacy development, assists the teacher in delivering effective instruction, and reports effectiveness data, it should be reviewed. But, it would not be prudent to assume that the curriculum will do all the work. On the contrary, a comprehensive plan must be developed for the systemic changes that will occur as the result of literacy intervention.

When reviewing curricula, it is also important to consider the skill level of implementing teachers relative to reading instruction. Expecting middle school and high school teachers to internalize and effectively deliver explicit reading instruction without extensive training and study is unrealistic. This is not to say that they won't make a valiant attempt. However, are we willing to subject our struggling students to trial-and-error instruction rather than review all materials and professional development that reading researchers and practitioners have developed for teachers of strategic and intensive learners?

Recognition of these facts allows the District Literacy Intervention Committee to review curricula with an open mind rather than look for something that seems familiar. Remember, more of the same will not help students who struggle. We've already tried that.

KEYS TO SUCCESS

- Review curricula and strategies that explicitly meet student need (i.e., strategic and intensive levels).
- Ask specific questions about how the curriculum addresses student need, including content, time, intensity, methodology, and training and exit criteria.
- Know the state and federal criteria for research-based intervention.
- Validate publisher claims with phone calls and/or e-mails to state consultants and professional references, and plan site visits to schools that are using the curriculum.
- Ask for and confirm effectiveness data on use and effectiveness in schools with similar demographics.
- Review training and support options and requirements as outlined by the publisher.
- Investigate the publisher's record on timely delivery and support.
- Know your district's ordering process; make friends with the Purchasing Department!

THE WORKSHEET

Use Worksheet 1.6 to review published curricula and to remind yourself of the types of information you need in order to make an informed decision about purchasing literacy intervention materials.

Worksheet 1.6 *Publisher Checklist*

Publisher _____ Curriculum _____

Contact information_____

Criteria	Yes	No	N/A	Comments	Reviewers
Age-appropriate					
English language learners					
General education					
Special education					
Appropriate for strategic learners.					
Appropriate for intensive learners.					
Systematic, explicit instruction based on current reading research.					
Includes comprehensive assessment.					
Meets the assessed need of students.					
Students place according to skill level.					
Validation					
Meets federal guidelines.					
Meets state guidelines.					
Reviewed effectiveness data.					
Meets district guidelines.					
Professional references have been checked.					
Site visits completed.					
Publisher claims checked.					
Training					
Includes research, background knowledge, content, and methodology.					
Additional professional development on teaching reading is available.					
References for quality of training are checked.					
Follow-up training is available.					
Coach's training is available.					
Training model includes paths that build internal capacity.					
Publisher maintains significant quality control of training.					
Implementation					
Publisher will consult regarding implementation, long-range planning, and data collection.					
Ordering					
1. Order placed.					
2. Board approval received.					
3. PO sent to publisher.					
4. Order is being tracked.					
5. Firm date of delivery.					
6. Plans for distribution set.					

Phase 1

Professional Development

THE CHALLENGE

Once a curriculum or strategies for strategic and intensive learners has been identified or developed, it is necessary to organize a professional development plan that will provide initial and ongoing training for all implementers. This includes training for teachers, administrators, and counselors. Professional development can be an expensive process and is often not considered when districts originally decide to adopt literacy intervention. This is an area in which we cannot skimp. We must acknowledge that teachers at the middle school and high school levels will not rush to discard their grade-level content instruction to teach intervention. High-quality training is essential because it will have a direct effect on teachers' skills and attitudes once they begin to teach literacy intervention. Garmston and Wellman (1999, p. 172) define efficacy as "knowing that one has the capacity to make a difference and being willing and able to do so." They go on to explain: "If individuals or groups feel little efficacy, then blame, withdrawal, and rigidity is likely to follow. But teachers with robust efficacy are likely to expend more energy in their work, persevere longer and set more challenging goals, and continue in the face of failure." If teachers agree to adopt new materials and/or strategies but do not change their practice and embrace the science that supports the instruction, their effort will be superficial, and eventually one more set of books will be relegated to the back of the closet.

THE SOLUTION

Quality professional development is crucial when considering the implementation of literacy intervention. Elmore (2004, p. 104) defines professional development as "the set of knowledge- and skill-building activities that raise the capacity of teachers and administrators to respond to external demands and engage in the improvement of practice and performance." Fullan (2001) notes that innovation is multidimensional and we must address three major components of the change: new instructional materials, new teaching methodology, and change in belief systems. As previously stated, middle school and high school teachers, administrators, and counselors may not have background knowledge in beginning literacy development. It is all new learning, and the anxiety level will be high. A trainer with expertise in delivering professional

"Each group [teachers, administrators, counselors] is responsible for an aspect of implementing literacy intervention and, therefore, must understand how it will affect their practice."

development, curriculum components, literacy content, and knowledge of the challenges that face teachers will be able to initiate changes in belief systems and garner support for literacy intervention.

Additionally, professional development must fit the audience. Therefore, the training for teachers, administrators, and counselors will contain some common elements but will ultimately diverge to address the needs of each audience. Each group is responsible for an aspect of implementing literacy intervention and, therefore, must understand how it will affect their practice. It is, perhaps, more expensive to include various types of training, but the investment will prove worthwhile when implementation begins.

KEYS TO SUCCESS

- Arrange separate training for strategic classes and intensive classes based on the unique components of each.
- Find a consultant/trainer who is certified and experienced in the particular curriculum or strategies to be employed.
- Consult publishers to arrange training, and secure a trainer. Be sure that the selected consultant has experience with your district configuration (e.g., middle school and/or high school education, rural, urban, year-round schedule).
- Train substitute teachers and paraprofessionals, if possible. Literacy intervention is not something a middle school or high school substitute teacher can just pick up and teach. We don't want to lose valuable time.
- Schedule at least one session after September for new hires.
- If your school is in a large district that requires numerous sessions, request a team of trainers that will be dedicated to the district to ensure a coherent message.
- Order training material early so that teachers have the necessary materials to fully participate in training.
- Designate a member of the District Literacy Intervention Committee to attend all training sessions. This representative can answer many implementation questions that cannot and should not be answered by the trainer.

For teachers:
- Training should include documented research, curriculum content, methodology, and ample time for practice, demonstration, assessment, implementation, and reflection.
- Training should be scheduled for the maximum amount of time possible based on the recommendations of the publisher for each type of intervention (i.e., strategic or intensive). The more time teachers have to understand the content and the demands of intervention, the more comfortable they will feel at the beginning of and during the implementation.
- The trainer should understand the unique challenges of middle school and high school education.

For administrators:
- Administrators should be trained prior to the beginning of implementation so that they can begin to develop school-site plans.

- Training content should include background research, terminology, curriculum content or strategies, assessment systems including placement and progress-monitoring, demonstration lessons with observation protocols, development of a school-site plan, teacher choice, collection and analysis of data, teacher support, development of master schedules to support literacy intervention, and parent involvement.
- Administrator training may be of shorter duration than teacher training.

For counselors:
- Counselors should be trained prior to the beginning of implementation so that they understand the importance of careful placement of intervention students.
- Content should include an overview of instruction, placement and movement of students according to data, and a procedure for entry into and exit from the curriculum.
- Counselor training may be of shorter duration than teacher training.

THE WORKSHEET

Use Worksheet 1.7 as a guide when arranging professional development for initial and follow-up training for teachers, administrators, counselors, paraeducators, substitute teachers, and parents. Sometimes, the logistics of training set the tone for implementation. For training costs and content considerations, refer to Worksheets 1.4b and 1.6.

District/School Training Checklist

Type of training: Initial ______ Follow-up ______ Assess… mar…

Training Task	Cost	Funds used	Person responsible		Notes
Schedule training dates.					
Book trainer(s).					
Book training site(s).					
Design and distribute notification.					
Arrange food.					
Arrange audiovisual equipment.					
Register participants.					
Purchase training materials.					
Set up training room(s).					
Copy/prepare evaluation materials.					
Appoint a school/district facilitator.					

1. RTI model
2. Intervention instruction – materials + methodology
3. Inclusion/504/ESL/accommodations

Phase 1

Section 1.8

Accountability

Part A: Mutual Accountability

THE CHALLENGE

Part of innovation is accountability from all stakeholders. We have learned through experience that anything not monitored is considered optional. Marzano, Waters, and McNulty (2005, p. 66) would consider district-wide literacy intervention a "second-order change." It is a significant departure from the norm at the middle school and high school levels. A large-scale adoption of literacy intervention will change the way that middle schools and high schools do business by requiring that they shift focus from content-centered instruction to student-centered. We are asking middle school and high school teachers to teach content and use methodology not included in their educational training. It requires a paradigm shift for middle schools and high schools in their operation relative to student placement, class scheduling, and awarding credit. In such a tenuous environment, how can intervention be monitored in a way that both provides support and demands accountability?

THE SOLUTION

Fullan (2001, pp. 91–92) describes the need for both pressure and support to ensure successful innovation: "Successful change projects always include elements of both pressure and support. Pressure without support leads to resistance and alienation; support without pressure leads to drift or waste of resources." Applied to a literacy intervention model, pressure and support focus on mutual accountability at all levels of the implementation with support mechanisms that enable the implementer to achieve the desired goal. For example, we cannot expect a site administrator to support literacy intervention without training and funds for the requisite materials. Conversely, we cannot provide ample support for an administrator who then looks the other way while the materials sit in the bookroom and teachers are told to ignore the district mandate. Therefore, it is up to the District Literacy Intervention Committee to determine the types of pressure and support that will result in accountability at all levels of literacy intervention.

In developing pressure and support for literacy intervention, it is helpful to use Elmore's (2004) "accountability for capacity" as a guideline. Elmore (p. 93) states: "Accountability must be a reciprocal process. For every increment of performance I demand from you, I have an equal responsibility to provide you with the capacity to meet the expectation. Likewise, for every investment you make in my skill and knowledge, I have a reciprocal responsibility to demonstrate some new increment in performance." Using the assertions of both Elmore and Fullan (2001), the District Literacy Intervention Committee must collaborate with school-site administrators and they, in turn, must collaborate with teachers to articulate the type of support necessary to implement literacy intervention with fidelity and accountability. This does not mean that the implementation of literacy intervention is negotiable. Collaboration simply allows the site administrator and the teachers to articulate their needs and thus promote ownership of the implementation plan.

KEYS TO SUCCESS

- The District Literacy Intervention Committee should already know the pressures (e.g., timely submission of data, classroom observations, cut points for screening, placement of students) that will be imposed.
- Allow both district and site administration to articulate what they will require in terms of funds, materials, training, and personnel for the successful implementation of literacy intervention.
- Itemize each district requirement with a corresponding support mechanism for site administration.
- Determine accountability for each item.
- Be reasonable about first-year expectations and the capacity for support.
- Revisit this document biannually or annually for necessary revisions and expansions.

THE WORKSHEETS

Refer to Worksheet 1.8a.1 as an example of documentation of mutual accountability that is needed at the district and site administrator levels. Use Worksheet 1.8a.2 to create a mutual accountability model for your district and site administration.

Phase 1

Worksheet 1.8a.1 *Mutual Accountability District/School-Site Administrators*

(sample)

"Accountability must be a reciprocal process. For every increment of performance I demand from you, I have an equal responsibility to provide you with the capacity to meet the expectation. Likewise, for every investment you make in my skill and knowledge, I have a reciprocal responsibility to demonstrate some new increment in performance. This is the principle of 'accountability for capacity' … " (Elmore, 2004)

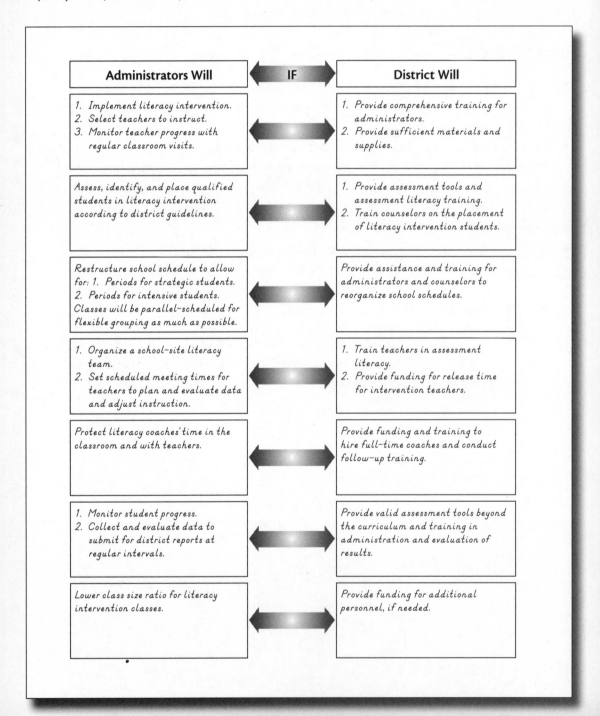

Administrators Will	IF	District Will
1. Implement literacy intervention. 2. Select teachers to instruct. 3. Monitor teacher progress with regular classroom visits.		1. Provide comprehensive training for administrators. 2. Provide sufficient materials and supplies.
Assess, identify, and place qualified students in literacy intervention according to district guidelines.		1. Provide assessment tools and assessment literacy training. 2. Train counselors on the placement of literacy intervention students.
Restructure school schedule to allow for: 1. Periods for strategic students. 2. Periods for intensive students. Classes will be parallel-scheduled for flexible grouping as much as possible.		Provide assistance and training for administrators and counselors to reorganize school schedules.
1. Organize a school-site literacy team. 2. Set scheduled meeting times for teachers to plan and evaluate data and adjust instruction.		1. Train teachers in assessment literacy. 2. Provide funding for release time for intervention teachers.
Protect literacy coaches' time in the classroom and with teachers.		Provide funding and training to hire full-time coaches and conduct follow-up training.
1. Monitor student progress. 2. Collect and evaluate data to submit for district reports at regular intervals.		Provide valid assessment tools beyond the curriculum and training in administration and evaluation of results.
Lower class size ratio for literacy intervention classes.		Provide funding for additional personnel, if needed.

Worksheet 1.8a.2 *Mutual Accountability District/School-Site Administrators*

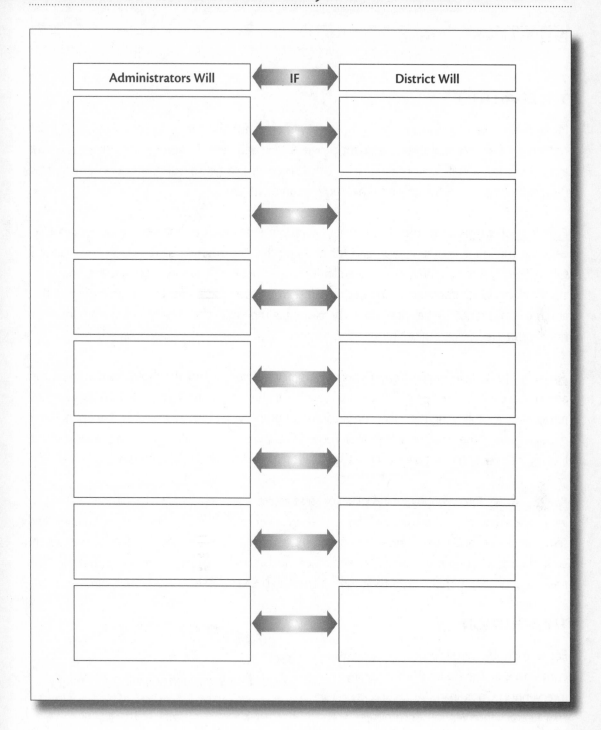

Phase 1

Part B: Monitoring Progress

THE CHALLENGE

Progress must be monitored on all levels. Literacy intervention will not be successful unless all stakeholders are held accountable for student progress. With numerous improvement projects on the agenda of most administrators and teachers, this becomes a sometimes arduous but necessary task. Progress monitoring is the only way that success can be measured.

**For district administration:** The District Literacy Intervention Committee is responsible for developing the implementation plan and for ensuring that site administrators act on the mandate. Often, literacy intervention is in the forefront of the district conversation until the next innovation comes along. Once implementation begins and seems to be progressing, less attention is paid to it and the implementation begins to drift. Therefore, it is imperative that the District Literacy Intervention Committee be part of the monitoring process.

**For school-site administration:** District plans include mechanisms that hold site administrators accountable for the success of literacy intervention at the school site. Again, site administrators are responsible for following the many innovations adopted by the district. It seems that there is not enough time in the day. The schedule of most site administrators is already so overwhelming that literacy intervention may take a back seat to issues that are seemingly more pressing.

**For teachers:** Intervention requires that we assess, adjust, and teach. Progress monitoring is an ongoing process that informs instruction. This is a departure from the common practice of quarterly and semester exams and a pass/fail approach to teaching at the middle school and high school levels; teachers at these levels must become familiar with collecting data and analyzing it to inform instruction. This means continually monitoring and adjusting instruction based on student academic progress.

THE SOLUTION

For district administration: Once again, we come back to the duties of the Literacy Intervention Coordinator and the District Literacy Intervention Committee. Their task does not end when implementation begins, nor after the first or second year. Literacy leadership must be dedicated positions that focus primarily on the implementation and sustainability of literacy intervention. The coordinator and the committee must maintain a visible presence with site

"Literacy leadership must be dedicated positions that focus primarily on the implementation and sustainability of literacy intervention. The [Literacy Intervention] coordinator and the [District Literacy Intervention] committee must maintain a visible presence with site administrators and teachers."

administrators and teachers. The perception that the district is no longer interested or supportive is the death knell for literacy intervention. The concept of pressure and support (Fullan, 2001) is, again, extremely helpful for accountability at the district level. Pressure and support for the District Literacy Intervention Committee provides an accountability measure that will guide its actions. For example, if the committee is required to report to the school board on a regular basis, it is more likely to invest the time, funds, and training necessary to ensure that the intervention is successful. Additionally, the committee should not wait until the board report to hold site administration accountable for instruction at the school site. Data collection and reporting should be part of principal meetings on a regular basis. The discussions of data must result in an action plan to improve implementation, instruction, and student scores.

KEYS TO SUCCESS: *District Administration*

- Develop a pressure and support document for the District Literacy Intervention Committee and the board of education or superintendent.
- Schedule one meeting per quarter/trimester with the school principals to focus on progress data for intervention students. Develop action plans with site administrators.
- Arrange for the District Literacy Intervention Committee to visit intervention classrooms at least once per quarter to demonstrate commitment and to obtain a realistic view of fidelity at school sites.
- Direct the District Literacy Intervention Committee to meet on a regular basis to review the long-term plan and make adjustments.

KEYS TO SUCCESS: *School-Site Administration*

Site administrators are a crucial part of the accountability process. They must be trained in the components of literacy intervention, understand what explicit instruction looks like in the classroom, and actively engage in the analysis of data with teachers. The value that the site administrator places on literacy intervention will be absorbed and reflected in the attitude of teachers and students. Reading instruction at the middle school and high school levels is not popular; we wish it weren't so! However, in many districts, more students read below grade-level than at grade-level. This issue will not disappear if we do not acknowledge it nor will it improve if literacy intervention is not implemented with full support from site administrators.

- Include implementation of literacy intervention in the site administrator's performance plan so that there will be concrete accountability.
- Commit to both formal and informal intervention classroom visits.
- Know what systematic instruction for strategic and intensive students should look like, and know what students should be able to do.
- Develop a master schedule with literacy intervention as a focal point and find opportunities for parallel-scheduling. Ensure that students are placed according to assessment in homogeneous, but flexible, groups. (Parallel schedules and flexible groups are discussed in Phase 2: Implementation.)
- Arrange time for intervention teachers to meet, review data, and adjust instruction based on that data.

KEYS TO SUCCESS: *Teachers*

Teachers have two major goals in teaching literacy intervention: (1) teach the curriculum and/or designated strategies with fidelity; and (2) adjust instruction based on student data. Student progress is a direct result of instruction and pacing. Teachers must be sufficiently trained in current reading research and how it pertains to adolescent literacy intervention. In fact, we cannot measure student progress without first making sure teachers are instructing intervention curricula as designed (Biancarosa & Snow, 2004). Teachers must also be trained in the process of data analysis and its impact on instruction. Coaching and classroom observation are both essential to monitoring teacher progress. Training and coaching will be discussed in more detail in a subsequent section. Teachers should:

- Meet on a regularly scheduled basis with an agenda that includes data review and planning based on student progress.
- Attend initial training and follow-up training, and work with coaches to refine practice techniques.
- Be prepared to be observed, formally and informally.

THE WORKSHEET

Use Worksheet 1.8b to help ensure that all stakeholders—the district, the site administrators, and the teachers—are accountable for student progress and success. This worksheet will serve as a record of accountability, beginning with initial training and progressing through the implementation and continuation stages of literacy intervention.

Worksheet 1.8b *Progress Monitoring Checklist*

Type of Progress	Verification	Due	Person Responsible
District Literacy Committee			
1. Attend training.			
2. Visit classrooms.			
3. Hold principal meetings.			
4. Present report to board.			
5. Hold District Literacy Intervention Committee meetings.			
Site Administration			
1. Attend training.			
2. Observe classrooms.			
3. Develop master schedule.			
4. Organize School Site Literacy Intervention Team.			
5. Schedule regular meeting times for intervention teachers.			
6. Collect ongoing assessment data from teachers.			
Teachers			
1. Attend training and follow-up.			
2. Teach with fidelity.			
3. Attend Site Literacy Intervention Team meetings.			
4. Adjust instruction based on data.			

Phase 1

Part C: Data Collection

THE CHALLENGE

Assessment should be a priority on the educational agendas of administrators and teachers. High-stakes testing abounds, and a district is measured by the progress of all its students. Additional assessment for intervention students may be seen as another task for teachers and students. Additionally, intervention is expensive in time, talent, and money. School boards and districts require information that demonstrates that students are making progress. Often, however, the only measure that counts is the high-stakes test results. Intensive- and strategic-intervention students are already performing below grade-level, so even two or three years' growth in reading may not alter the result of standardized assessment within a short period of time. For example, a student is in the ninth grade and reads at the second-grade level. The student is placed in intense intervention. Hypothetically, the student makes three years' growth in the first year. It sounds wonderful, and everyone is delighted with the progress. However, the student is still five years below the level of the standardized test that is now at the tenth-grade level; thus, the standardized data is less likely to show significant growth. The challenge is how to demonstrate growth in reading achievement and, at the same time, satisfy the political need to show progress on grade-level standardized assessment.

Once a district/school puts intervention in place, student progress will depend on how well the teacher follows the prescriptive instruction and design of the chosen curriculum. If a teacher closes the door and reads aloud from the grade-level text, we cannot expect that students will demonstrate the acquisition of literacy skills. Student progress cannot be measured without also assessing whether teachers are adhering to the instructional design of the intervention curriculum.

An additional challenge is that schools have developed some knowledge regarding the collection of data. Changing instruction based on data is, in many cases, still the missing link. Analysis of data—placement, formative, and summative—is an activity that requires expertise. Teachers must know when and how to adjust instruction. Once students are placed into intervention, it is unacceptable to move through instruction and assume that students are making progress without documentation. Although teachers can collect anecdotal data, it is not specific enough to adjust instruction to meet the needs of the students. As Lyon (2006) states: "Teachers' decisions should be based on strong evidenced-based knowledge, not beliefs, philosophies, untested assumptions, or anecdotes. Evidence is not the plural of anecdote." In the intervention classroom, formative assessment must be collected and analyzed on a regular basis. Summative assessment and progress monitoring are also crucial to measure if we want to know if students are meeting learning objectives and progressing toward grade-level.

THE SOLUTION

Remember that literacy intervention is not just buying books and assigning students. The goal in designing a comprehensive literacy plan is to acknowledge and account for the progression of skill and implementation on the part of the administrator, teacher, and student.

Elmore (2004, p. 254) asserts: "Improvement is a process, not an event. Schools don't suddenly 'get better' and meet their performance targets. Schools build capacity by generating internal accountability—greater agreement and coherence on expectations for teachers and students—and then by working their way through the problems of instructional practice at ever-increasing levels of complexity and demand." The crucial part of Elmore's statement relative to literacy intervention

> *"The crucial part of Elmore's [2004] statement relative to literacy intervention encourages administrators and teachers to recognize that improvement does not occur overnight. It is a process, and to go through the process, districts need a plan that includes accountability at all levels."*

encourages administrators and teachers to recognize that improvement does not occur overnight. It is a process, and to go through the process, districts need a plan that includes accountability at all levels.

Formative and summative assessment. Systematic, explicit literacy intervention must include formative assessment at regular intervals that allow teachers to adjust instruction in a timely manner. Formative assessment is based on learning objectives and how well students transfer that knowledge to various formats. This provides an opportunity for teachers to differentiate instruction within the class. Summative assessment is a cumulative measure that indicates growth based on the content of instruction. Both formative and summative assessments must be administered if we are to measure whether literacy intervention is effective (Biancarosa & Snow 2004).

Progress monitoring to show reading growth. Progress monitoring assessments are valid and reliable standardized assessments that are either norm-referenced or criterion-referenced. They measure a student's progress outside the curriculum, and data can be analyzed statistically to show whether student progress is significant. For literacy intervention, progress monitoring should include, but not be limited to, assessment in fluency and comprehension.

KEYS TO SUCCESS

- Inventory the types of standardized tests the district/school already uses to determine if the tests are appropriate for showing reading growth.
- Ask the curriculum consultant or the publisher to recommend valid and reliable assessments.
- Look for assessments that are group-administered and easy to score. (These types of assessments are less likely for fluency, but probable for comprehension.)
- Administer progress-monitoring assessments pre-instruction and post-instruction, either annually or semiannually.
- Analyze data immediately so that the results will inform placement and instruction.
- Include progress-monitoring assessments in public reports to school boards, staff, and parents.

Progress monitoring to show growth relative to grade-level standards. As previously explained, demonstrating growth toward grade-level is especially difficult for intensive-intervention students, but it may be required by boards of education and parent groups. Given this political reality, it is important to analyze and share this data with careful explanation and presentation. We cannot

Phase 1

expect students who are reading significantly below grade-level to suddenly perform at benchmark levels. Learning to read is a process that takes time. Remember that intervention begins at the functioning level of the student. This is a critical message to convey to those who are not in the field of education or who may not be knowledgeable about reading intervention research.

Certainly, it is also important to keep track of the progress that students are making toward grade-level. If we are working with students in the lowest percentiles, our ultimate goal is to demonstrate that students are moving toward grade-level. The operative word here is "moving."

Based on standardized assessments, students across the country are grouped into performance categories. Many states use a three-tier model in which students are identified as performing at benchmark, strategic, or intensive levels. In California for example, students are grouped into five categories based on their performance on the criterion-referenced California Standards Test: (1) far below basic; (2) below basic; (3) basic; (4) proficient; and (5) advanced. Students are assessed annually, and their scores place them in one of the five categories. Whichever rating system a state uses, it is vital to identify students who are performing at proficient levels and students whose scores indicate the need for assistance.

Much focus is placed on whether student scores are rising and on corresponding numerical values of increase. Rather than show percentage points of student progress, it is more informative in an intervention system to show movement toward higher levels of performance. Using the example of California performance categories, Figure 1.8a shows hypothetical initial levels of students in intense intervention and their movement toward higher levels of achievement after one year.

Figure 1.8a *Moving toward proficiency*

School Year	Far Below Basic	Below Basic	Basic	Proficient	Advanced
2005	70%	30%	0	0	0
2006	30%	45%	20%	5%	0

Clearly, not all students move out of the "far below basic" level in the first year. Each band represents a range of performance, so it will take students at the low end of the range longer to show movement to the high end. However, the hypothetical data shows that students are beginning to show progress in student achievement relative to grade-level assessments. The percentage of students in the lowest category has decreased, and the percentage of students in the second band has increased, showing movement toward proficiency. Twenty percent of students in the "below basic" category have moved to the "basic" category. Although there are still students in the "far below basic" category, movement to the right shows overall progress. This type of presentation, along with explanation, is beneficial when presenting grade-level data for intervention students. Whatever the student performance categories, movement to the right—along with progress-monitoring data that demonstrates incremental growth in reading—will provide a more complete picture of student achievement, the validity of instruction, and the effectiveness of the literacy intervention plan.

KEYS TO SUCCESS

- Explain the difference between grade-level assessment and multilevel assessment to all stakeholders at the beginning of the intervention.
- Determine how data will be presented to the public.
- When determining needs of students, make sure that their current percentile/category is listed so that it can be compared to the subsequent test.
- Do not get discouraged if students do not initially show growth. Keep in mind that the first year of instruction is a learning year for everyone.

THE WORKSHEET

Use Worksheet 1.8c as a template to identify and monitor the collection of: (1) curriculum-based data; (2) pre- and post-assessments (for measuring progress independent of a curriculum); and (3) state standardized assessments. Remember, if you do not monitor administration and collection of data, effective analysis and response will suffer.

Worksheet 1.8c *District/School Training Checklist*

Type of Data	Measurement	Date administered	Due date	Person responsible for data collection	Notes
Placement					
Formative assessment					
Summative assessment					
Progress Monitoring					
1. Pretest					
2. Posttest					
3. Standardized tests (state/local)					

Part D: Assessment Literacy

THE CHALLENGE

Data must be collected and analyzed. Teachers must adjust instruction based on the information they learn from those analyses. Teachers are already overwhelmed and are now expected to teach groups of struggling students. Administrators are primarily concerned with grade-level data and are anxious for students to do well on state assessments. The pressure is high. Literacy intervention requires close attention to data. It is imperative that administrators and teachers not only know how to administer the selected assessments but also know what to do with the data once they collect it.

THE SOLUTION

Assessment literacy is the vehicle that enables teachers and administrators to examine student progress and to make informed decisions about possible changes in instruction. Fullan (2001, p. 127) outlines three capacities that define assessment literacy, two of which apply to literacy intervention: (1) the capacity to examine student performance data and results (i.e., to make critical sense of the data); and (2) the capacity to act on this understanding by developing classroom and school improvement plans in order to make the kinds of changes needed to increase literacy performance.

> *"Data analysis serves as a vehicle for the [District Literacy Intervention] committee to review teacher fidelity, administrative support, and student placement."*

Assessment literacy is critical for three reasons. First, we cannot afford to assume that students are learning. This is the last chance for middle school and high school students to gain crucial literacy skills that contribute to life-long choices and success. Second, assessment results also measure the effectiveness of an implementation plan. Are all stakeholders following the implementation plan, and is that adherence reflected in student achievement? Third, the District Literacy Intervention Committee must determine if the intervention curriculum is meeting the needs of the students. Data analysis serves as a vehicle for the committee to review teacher fidelity, administrative support, and student placement. If all elements are functional yet students are not making progress, it might be time to rethink the choice of intervention. It is important to note that it takes time for all of the elements to be put in place and function cohesively. Remember that school improvement is a process; don't jump to conclusions with the first set of student data. However, if students are not making measurable progress over time, it is imperative to adjust the plan or to examine the choice of intervention.

KEYS TO SUCCESS

- Include assessment literacy as part of the professional development plan at the initial stage of placement, and then once again when teachers have had a chance to work with the intervention curriculum and students.
- Train administrators, teachers, and counselors. Counselors are often left out of the equation, yet they may be the individuals responsible for assigning students to classes.
- Once implementation is underway, require that teachers report data to the principal at regular intervals. The principal should then report the data to the District Literacy Intervention Committee.

THE WORKSHEETS

Use Worksheet 1.8d to think about and create a plan for developing an assessment literacy plan at the school site, then use Worksheet 1.8e to develop your own plan. Because intervention requires close attention to student progress, a specific plan increases the likelihood of data analysis and response.

Worksheet 1.8d *Assessment Literacy Checklist for Literacy Intervention*

(sample)

Task	How to accomplish	Completion date and/or Ongoing
Teachers, administrators, and counselors are trained in the administration, scoring, and interpretation of placement, formative, and progress-monitoring assessments.		
Teachers and administrators submit to the District Literacy Intervention Committee a student performance data-collection and analysis plan at each school site.		
Teachers, administrators, and counselors have scheduled monthly meetings to analyze and discuss ongoing student performance data, how it relates to instruction, and how it informs the instructional and pacing plan.		
Teachers and administrators have access to support personnel to assist with data analysis, how it relates to instruction, and how it informs the instructional and pacing plan.		
Teachers, administrators, and counselors have access to support personnel to assist with adjusting instructional plans and placement of students.		
Teachers and administrators submit a yearly student performance data report and an improvement plan based on student progress-monitoring data.		
Student performance data is shared with staff and parents.		

Phase 1

Worksheet 1.8e *Assessment Literacy Checklist for Literacy Intervention*

Task	How to accomplish	Completion date and/or Ongoing

Implementation

PHASE 2: *Implementation*

The second phase of literacy reform is implementation. Fullan (2001, p. 69) describes implementation as "the process of putting into practice an idea, program, or set of activities and structures new to the people attempting or expecting to change." This phase occurs over the first two to three years of implementing literacy intervention. It is a time when teachers and administrators begin to put theory into practice. It is unrealistic to assume that all implementers will wholeheartedly embrace the notion of literacy intervention at the middle school and high school levels, but with support, practice, and accountability, belief systems will begin to change. Teachers and students see progress, and administrators watch test scores rise. However, it is a process that requires time, effort, and clarity of purpose. Fullan (p. 92) identifies what he refers to as an "implementation dip": "Things get worse before they get better and clearer as people grapple with the meaning and skills of change. The relationship between behavioral and belief change is reciprocal and ongoing, with change in doing or behavior a necessary experience on the way to breakthroughs in meaning and understanding." Even with the best initiation planning, implementers will experience bumps in the road. This is expected—even preferred—because it informs the process of improvement.

The phases of reform are certainly not finite. The plans and activities of the initiation phase affect the implementation phase and the continuance phase. The implementation phase offers the opportunity to discover if the initial literacy plan meets the needs of the teachers, students, and administrators or if the plan requires refinement. Therefore, it is beneficial to think of the process as a continuum, resulting in a dynamic plan that defines and redefines the application of literacy intervention. The implementation phase, then, offers a great opportunity to learn and improve. As Elmore (2000, p. 25) observes: "Organizations that improve do so because they create and nurture agreement on what is worth achieving, and they set in motion the internal processes by which people progressively learn how to do what they need to do in order to achieve what is worthwhile."

The following sections describe the steps of the plan that address the actual implementation of literacy intervention at the school site. Lyon (2006) describes the critical nature of site implementation: "If you find a program isn't doing well, that is to be expected if teachers aren't implementing the program with fidelity. Likewise, you can have the most well trained teacher, but if the program is ineffective, kids will not learn. One can also have a great teacher and a great program, but if the building-level leadership is poor and the teachers are not provided enough time to teach and collaborate with one another, then kids will not learn. It is complex, but so is life. The point is when all elements are in place, students learn—even those from the direst circumstances." The implementation phase is the crucial time when all the elements begin to fall into place. The discussion around continued instructional improvement in literacy intervention reflects reality when we add students to the mix. What occurs during this time will determine if literacy intervention is a passing fad or a sustainable innovation that will help struggling students.

Awareness— Setting the Stage

THE CHALLENGE

Everyone has agreed that struggling readers need help and initial plans have been developed. However, while middle school and high school teachers will admit that many of their students are struggling readers, they will not necessarily volunteer to teach the lowest performers. Many will claim that teaching reading is not their job and go on to say that this should have been taken care of in elementary school. Once the news is out, rumors begin. Teachers may feel threatened by the new approach. Resistance may begin before literacy intervention is ever implemented. Elmore (2000, p. 29) expresses one of the common resistance mechanisms relative to innovation: "Educators are fond of responding to any piece of research that demonstrates a promising approach, or any seemingly successful example from practice with a host of reasons why 'it'—whatever 'it' is—would never work in *their* setting. *Their* students are much different from those in the example, *their* communities would never tolerate such practices, *their* union contract contains very different provisions that would never permit such actions, *their* teachers are much too sophisticated (or unsophisticated) to deal with such improvements … "

Without fully understanding the need, components, and support, teachers and administrators may begin to shut down to the idea of systematic instruction in reading. They may also view literacy as one more in a long line of doomed reforms. Fullan (2001, p. 81) articulates the stance of many teachers when he observes: "Teachers and others know enough now, if they didn't 20 years ago, not to take change seriously unless the central administrators demonstrate through actions that they should." Therefore, one of the most formidable obstacles to innovation is misinformation. The sooner everyone is informed, the better.

THE SOLUTION

Awareness sessions for school staff and parents are a first step to garnering support from the stakeholders. Awareness sessions provide opportunities to bring to everyone's attention student needs based on data, the intervention plan (including mutual accountability), and the literacy curriculum. It is important at this point to be prepared for, and to listen to, dissenters. Questions and concerns voiced by critics can offer valuable insight into

"Questions and concerns voiced by critics can offer valuable insight into what others may be thinking and may help the District Literacy Intervention Committee to refine the implementation plan as needed."

what others may be thinking and may help the District Literacy Intervention Committee to refine the implementation plan if needed. Entertaining various viewpoints does not mean that the plan should be abandoned or so watered down that students do not receive the instruction necessary to raise literacy levels and teachers are not held accountable. Taking others' opinions into consideration simply means that listening to all voices may inform the implementation plan and promote collaboration to develop accountability and capacity.

KEYS TO SUCCESS

- Ensure that the District Literacy Intervention Team attends all awareness sessions.
- Present current school and district data that portrays the extent of the literacy problem across all student populations (i.e., general education, special education, ELLs).
- Schedule a comprehensive overview of the components of the literacy intervention curriculum for strategic and intensive students, and have the overview presented by someone who can address content and implementation questions.
- Prepare a list of professional references and effectiveness data pertaining to the intervention curriculum or strategies employed.
- Prepare a list of sites that teachers can visit to see the intervention in action.
- Prepare a detailed plan for assessment, including placement and progress monitoring.
- Prepare a detailed plan that outlines the timeline, training, materials, accountability, and support for teachers, including entry and exit criteria for students.
- Arrange for teachers and site administrators to meet to identify needs that will assist them in teaching the intervention with fidelity.
- Prepare a document of frequently asked questions, which may include answers to the following questions teachers may ask:
    - ✦ Will we receive enough materials for all students, including consumable materials?
    - ✦ Will we be able to reorder materials, including consumable materials and teaching supplies?
    - ✦ Will we receive training? Will training take place during school time or personal time?
    - ✦ Will we have time to meet and plan at the school site?
    - ✦ Will we have support at the school site in the form of coaches and/or follow-up training?
    - ✦ How can we be sure that the intervention class will not become a dumping ground for students who can read but have behavior problems?
    - ✦ Will teachers have a say in the development and composition of the intervention class?
    - ✦ Will students be held accountable for grade-level Language Arts in addition to the intervention?
    - ✦ How does the intervention help students pass standardized tests?
    - ✦ My administrator wants to see state standards on the class agenda when I teach. Will administrators be trained and will they understand the intervention?
    - ✦ How will students be placed?
    - ✦ How does the intervention address the needs of general education, special needs, and ELL students?
    - ✦ Will we be evaluated on classroom instruction and student progress?

- How do we grade students?
- What if my students are not motivated to read?
- Who is going to teach intervention? How are assignments going to be determined?
- What is the class size?
- Will students in each class be grouped by ability and language acquisition?

THE WORKSHEET

Use Worksheet 2.1 to prepare for each group that will receive an awareness or progress session. This worksheet functions as a checklist for developing a plan and as a guide for adding and deleting items as necessary.

Phase 2

Worksheet 2.1 *Awareness/Progress Session Checklist*

Task	Date	Person responsible	Notes
Arrange overview with a qualified presenter.			
Compile current student data for a report.			
Prepare FAQ document.			
Identify date, time, and location of session.			
Obtain sample materials for review by parents and teachers.			
Announce the session at least one month in advance.			
Invite administrators, counselors, teachers, and parents.			
Book audiovisual equipment.			
Order food and drink, if applicable.			

The Role of the Site Administrator

THE CHALLENGE

The role of the site administrator (e.g., the principal, the assistant principal) is critical to the success of any innovation, including literacy intervention. As the instructional leader, the administrator implements the district literacy intervention plan. Site administrators cannot do their job if district administrators are not actively supportive, and teachers cannot do their job if site administrators are not actively supportive. The attitude and involvement of the site administrator sets the tone at the school, and teachers reflect that tone. Site administrators are bombarded with various innovations and are expected to be all things to all people. Intervention students may spend much of their time in the administrator's office and may also be the group that is keeping the school from achieving its academic progress goals. Convincing teachers to embrace a group of struggling students and learn new content is a big job. The site administrator will ultimately decide, by example, whether literacy intervention is a priority or merely an afterthought at the school site. As Fullan (2001, p. 78) asserts: "The principal has always been the 'gatekeeper' of change, often determining the fate of innovations coming from the outside or from teacher initiatives on the inside."

THE SOLUTION

Site administrators must make the decision to embrace intervention, whether they philosophically agree with it or not. The staff and students are keenly aware of the opinions of their school's administrators. It is unfair to teachers and students to half-heartedly implement literacy intervention. Children's futures are at stake. The site administrator can take steps to ensure success at the school site by implementing literacy intervention as outlined in the district plan, by beginning important conversations around instruction and data, and by supporting the teachers charged with delivering the curriculum. The responsibilities of the administrator relative to literacy intervention are outlined on the following page.

> *"It is unfair to teachers and students to half-heartedly implement literacy intervention. Children's futures are at stake."*

Phase 2

KEYS TO SUCCESS

- Choose teachers wisely.
- Delegate: Form a School-Site Literacy Intervention Team.
- Collaborate with teachers to develop school-site mutual accountability document.
- Work with the School-Site Literacy Intervention Team to collect, analyze, and act upon data.
- Be a cheerleader. Support and applaud the intervention effort with students, teachers, and parents.
- Take the time to learn about the chosen literacy curriculum and strategies. Attend initial training and follow-up sessions.
- Nurture by listening to teachers' doubts, fears, and constructive ideas. This is new for everyone.
- Lead in the acquisition of materials by making sure that orders are placed on time and materials are ready when classes begin.
- Work with the District Literacy Intervention Committee and the School-Site Literacy Intervention Team to develop schedules that promote flexible, homogeneous groups.
- Observe the literacy intervention classrooms on a regular basis.
- Evaluate teacher skills in the literacy intervention classes.
- Report student progress to students, staff, parents, and teachers.
- Create a culture of literacy at the school site.
- Apply pressure and provide support for literacy intervention.

THE WORKSHEET

Use Worksheet 2.2 to perform the tasks necessary for administrative support of literacy intervention. (Tasks that are marked with an asterisk must be performed by the principal or principal designee; the remaining tasks may be performed by the administrator or a member of the School-Site Literacy Intervention Team.)

Worksheet 2.2 *Site Administrator Checklist*

Task	Date	Person responsible	Notes
*Attend awareness sessions.			
*Attend literacy intervention training.			
*Choose literacy intervention teachers.			
*Create School-Site Literacy Intervention Team.			
Assess students for placement.			
Hold awareness sessions for staff and parents.			
*Develop master schedule that reflects parallel-scheduling and homogeneous groups.			
*Counselors attend training.			
Prepare orders for instructional materials and relevant supplies.			
*Observe literacy intervention classrooms.			
*Schedule regular meeting time with literacy intervention teachers.			
Organize additional training needed for teachers.			
*Collect and analyze ongoing assessment data from literacy intervention teachers.			
*Identify and hire a literacy intervention coach.			
*Meet with School-Site Literacy Intervention Team to analyze data and adjust instruction.			

* This task must be performed by the principal or principal designee.

Phase 2

Choosing Teachers

THE CHALLENGE

As previously stated, middle school and high school teachers are not trained to teach reading. They invested themselves in specific content to be shared with willing and enthusiastic students who could read and understand grade-level material. Instead, they find themselves in classrooms where students struggle to read and comprehend.

Student outcome in literacy intervention is largely dependent on the skill of the teacher. If our struggling readers could teach themselves, they wouldn't need intervention. Explicit literacy instruction requires that teachers learn new content and methodology. It is "on-your-feet" teaching; instruction must be direct, systematic, and diagnostic. As if that is not enough, adolescent students in literacy intervention may have developed negative behavior patterns to mask their difficulties with reading. Granzin (2006) describes an emotional withdrawal experienced by many struggling readers: "… you can almost watch children who are struggling begin to turn off and exhibit behaviors that are going to interfere with their learning, beginning to develop a set of defensive postures. Sometimes it looks like 'I don't care,' sometimes it looks like 'I am interested in anything but this.' It [resistance] can take a lot of different forms, but nonetheless you can see kids do whatever they need to do to protect themselves." So the tough question for the site administrator is: Who will take this job?

THE SOLUTION

Clearly, conducting literacy intervention is not for the fainthearted. Choose intervention teachers wisely. We often hear that students with the most need deserve the best teachers. However, the best advanced-placement teacher may not necessarily be the best intervention teacher. Identify teachers who work well with struggling students. This does not mean that the teachers expect less from the students; on the contrary, expectations are high, but the teacher is willing and able to support students through the intense instruction they will receive and to deal with reluctant learners.

"We often hear that students with the most need deserve the best teachers. However, the best advanced-placement teacher may not necessarily be the best intervention teacher."

Have faith in your teachers. Most teachers choose education as a career because they want to make a difference. Years of trying to teach sophisticated concepts to students who cannot read well enough to negotiate a grade-level textbook is discouraging at best. Teaching literacy intervention may be just the spark that reignites a teacher's passion for instruction.

A key quality for an intervention teacher is endurance. These teachers must break through the emotional barriers that students have developed in response to their academic failure. Consider providing incentives for intervention teachers such as smaller class size, planning time, instructional aides, a classroom library, stipends, or making intervention a specialty.

KEYS TO SUCCESS

Choose teachers who:
- Work well with struggling students.
- Believe that all students can, and deserve to, learn to read and write.
- Have good organizational skills.
- Demonstrate good classroom-management skills.
- Are open to new content and instructional methodology.
- Already apply direct-instruction methodology in their content classes.
- Change instruction based on student performance data.
- Are willing to accept coaching.
- Do not stigmatize literacy intervention by creating a situation in which "those teachers" teach "those kids."

THE WORKSHEET

Use Worksheet 2.3 to help you evaluate potential literacy intervention teachers. Successful candidates need not meet all of the criteria, but you're looking for teachers who possess many of these qualities.

Phase 2

Worksheet 2.3 *Choosing Intervention Teachers*

Candidate teacher _____ Date _____

Qualities	Yes/No	Notes
Believes that all children can learn to read and write.		
Has good organizational skills.		
Has good classroom management and behavior management skills.		
Is able to accept coaching.		
Works well with others.		
Has good communication skills.		
Continuously refines teaching practices based on student progress.		
Works well with struggling students.		
Continuously monitors student progress.		
Is willing to try new instructional methodologies.		
Works well with parents.		
Welcomes administrator observation and participation.		

The School-Site Literacy Intervention Team

THE CHALLENGE

The principal is the instructional leader at the school site. The principal is also the plant manager, staff manager, budget director, and resident counselor. The implementation of literacy intervention additionally falls to the principal to organize, schedule, select teachers, and monitor instruction. However, literacy is not the principal's only instructional charge. He/she is also expected to know and understand the research and curriculum for each discipline. Managing all of these concurrent tasks sounds unmanageable, and sometimes proves to be the case. As a result, literacy may become just another "add-on" rather than a priority at the school.

THE SOLUTION

Fullan (2003, p. 38) asserts: "We need instead, leaders at many levels. Part and parcel of sustainability in organizations is the way in which they constantly spawn leadership and commitment in all quarters by fostering the flourishing of the intelligence, purpose, and passion of all members of the organization." Fullan calls for an instructional leader who recognizes that others on staff can help, and thus distributes leadership to those whose expertise and passion will assist in the implementation and sustainability of literacy intervention. Literacy coaches and intervention teachers can form the core of a School-Site Literacy Intervention Team. Coaches and teachers have a large stake in literacy intervention and therefore should contribute to the organization and monitoring of the implementation. If they own it, they will do a better job of implementation.

"Literacy coaches and intervention teachers can form the core of a School-Site Literacy Intervention Team."

KEYS TO SUCCESS

- Include intervention teachers, reading coaches, counselors, content-area teachers, and parents in assembling a School-Site Literacy Intervention Team.
- Provide a regularly scheduled meeting time for the team.

Phase 2

- Define the duties of the School-Site Literacy Intervention Team, which may include:
  - ✦ Assess and place students.
  - ✦ Develop schedules that allow for homogeneous groups and parallel schedules.
  - ✦ Determine content for strategic reading classes and excess time in intensive literacy classes.
  - ✦ Review student progress data and develop instructional plans for students who need additional help.
  - ✦ Confirm placement and exit criteria.
  - ✦ Inform the principal about professional development needs.
  - ✦ Develop information sessions for content-area teachers and parents.
  - ✦ Assist each other in refining instructional practice.
  - ✦ Initiate orders for instructional and library materials.

THE WORKSHEET

Use Worksheet 2.4 as a guide for developing tasks for the School-Site Literacy Intervention Team. The items listed are those necessary for successful implementation of literacy intervention. Your team may think of additional items that would enhance successful implementation at your school.

Worksheet 2.4 *School-Site Literacy Intervention Team Checklist*

Task	Due date	Person responsible	Notes
Administer screening and placement assessments and interpret results.			
Administer second screening and placement.			
Compile data and determine the number of classes needed for strategic and intensive students.			
Schedule literacy intervention awareness sessions for the entire staff and parents.			
Schedule assessment literacy training for intervention teachers.			
Inform parents of students identified as needing intervention.			
Schedule behavior management training for intervention teachers.			
Schedule inclusion training for special education and general education teachers.			
Schedule monthly meetings for literacy intervention teachers to discuss student progress data.			
Schedule follow-up sessions for literacy intervention teachers.			
Develop a plan to disseminate data to school staff and parents.			
Compile orders for instructional materials and classroom supplies.			
Develop a library order of high-interest/low-level independent reading books for literacy intervention classrooms.			
Meet monthly to analyze student data and adjust instruction.			
Meet quarterly to determine if students should be moved laterally based on data.			
Identify and recruit more teachers for literacy intervention.			

Phase 2

Student Placement and School-Site Schedules

THE CHALLENGE

The district has encouraged schools to develop a two-period parallel schedule for intense literacy intervention and a one-period class for strategic intervention. In this configuration, intervention classes are taught at the same time of the day. A parallel schedule results in the ability to move students from one group to another as indicated by their progress, and additional periods of instruction provide the time that struggling students need to make adequate progress toward grade-level achievement. However, struggling students are not the only group of students in the school. In fact, they may be a small group within the entire student population. Two periods for intensive students and an extra literacy class for strategic students demands thoughtful scheduling.

Various levels of student skill will exist within each intervention group. Students in need of intervention do not come to us as blank slates. They have learned some skills, but perhaps not the same set of skills. The administrator will also have to account for ELLs, special education students, and general education students when making scheduling decisions. Correct placement of students is crucial to success. Literacy intervention is not a one-size-fits-all solution. How does the site administrator meet the needs of the entire student body?

THE SOLUTION

The development of a schedule to meet the needs of struggling readers will, in fact, disrupt the status quo of middle school and high school. We have, for too long, let struggling students languish in classes in which they cannot read and comprehend the material. Often they give up or drop out. As Granzin (2006) points out: "Why aren't we pulling out all the stops and saying, 'Wait a minute. If you don't learn to read, there are so many disastrous consequences.' It would not be a good idea for kids never to get their early grounding in science or social studies, but I don't know that the life consequences would be anywhere nearly as dramatic as they are for kids who don't learn to read." Literacy intervention may be the last chance for middle school and high school students to learn literacy skills that will serve them for a lifetime.

"Parallel schedules allow for homogeneous grouping of students with similar skill levels and also allow teachers to move a student laterally among classes based on student assessments."

Intervention classes should be parallel-scheduled to allow for flexible student groupings. Parallel schedules allow for homogeneous grouping of students with similar skill levels and also allow teachers to move a student laterally among classes based on student assessments. In this configuration, a student receives the instruction needed, but if the student is moved, his/her entire class program will not have to be changed. Changing the master schedule is a significant undertaking. Developing parallel schedules around literacy intervention classes is difficult initially, but the benefits for teachers, students, counselors, and administrators far outweigh the challenges. Figure 2.1 provides an illustration of the benefits of parallel schedules for literacy intervention.

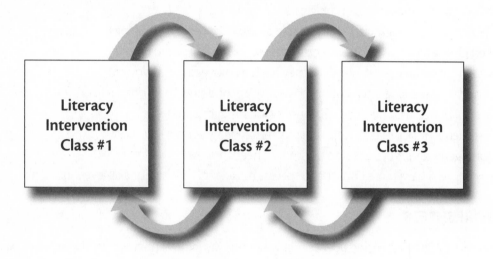

Figure 2.1 *Parallel schedules with lateral movement of students*

KEYS TO SUCCESS

- Work with the School-Site Literacy Intervention Team to assess and place students and to develop parallel schedules.
- Determine which students are eligible for literacy intervention based on district/school guidelines, standardized test scores, and student grades.
- Carefully assess students, and place them according to assessed need.
- Group students according to need:
  + Strategic students need *targeted* literacy instruction.
  + Intensive students need *comprehensive* literacy instruction.
- Strategic classes:
  + Place students with like needs in the same class, and clearly articulate the content of the class.
  + Strategic intervention requires a literacy class in addition to the grade-level Language Arts.
- Intensive classes:
  + Homogeneously group students with similar skill levels.
  + Two periods of intensive literacy serve as replacements for grade-level Language Arts and one other subject/elective. The goal is for students to achieve a literacy level that will allow them to access grade-level material in the shortest amount of time. (Literacy intervention should not be a life sentence!)
  + ELL students with minimal oral English receive a third period of instruction for oral academic English.

- Place students by assessment, not label:
  - ✦ Special education, general education, and ELLs may be placed in the same intervention class based on assessed needs. (Placement for special education students depends on the criteria in their individual education plan [IEP].)
  - ✦ Homogenously group ELLs with minimal oral English to allow for sheltered instruction and oral academic English.
  - ✦ Intervention classes may be multigrade.
- Parallel-schedule as many classes as possible to allow for flexible groupings:
  - ✦ Even just two parallel-scheduled classes allow for flexible groupings.
  - ✦ Students may be moved laterally if they need to move faster or slower.
  - ✦ Consider scheduling intervention classes for second and third or third and fourth periods. (School punctuality may not be a priority for struggling students.)
- Place students by skill level that has been determined by assessment scores:
  - ✦ Homogeneous groups ensure that student needs are met.
  - ✦ Teachers will have more impact and success if students have similar skill levels in a class.

THE WORKSHEETS

Use Worksheet 2.5a to list each student and his/her specific information, scores, and possible placement in intervention. Completing this list will assist in determining the number of students and classes for scheduling purposes. (Refer back to Worksheets 1.5c and 1.5d to compile additional relevant information). Use Worksheet 2.5b to guide the development of a master schedule that prioritizes literacy intervention.

Worksheet 2.5a *Student Placement Form*

School _____   Teacher _____   Grade _____

Student Name	Gen. Ed.	Sp. Ed.	ELL	Standardized test score	Secondary screening	Qualifies for intervention S = strategic I = intensive	Curriculum placement assessment	Placement in curriculum
1.								
2.								
3.								
4.								
5.								
6.								
7.								
8.								
9.								
10.								
11.								
12.								
13.								
14.								
15.								
16.								
17.								
18.								
19.								
20.								
21.								
22.								

Phase 2

Worksheet 2.5b *Master Schedule Criteria*

Item	Strategic	Intensive	Notes
Number of students			
Student-teacher ratio			
Number of periods of instruction			
Number of classes to be scheduled			
Number of teachers needed for instruction			
Possible positioning of classes, with one period for strategic students and two periods for intensive students (e.g., first and second periods, third and fourth periods)			
Number of classes that can be parallel-scheduled to allow for flexible grouping			
Number of common planning periods for intervention teachers to meet and plan			

Confirmation of Placement

THE CHALLENGE

Even with careful placement and scheduling, it is possible to incorrectly place students. Once instruction has begun, teacher observation informs the placement process. For instance, a teacher may believe that one or more students read well enough to be removed from intensive or strategic intervention. Conversely, a grade-level teacher may believe that a student in his/her classroom requires intervention. Both teachers' data is largely anecdotal. Ultimately, student placement decisions are left to the School-Site Literacy Intervention Team and site administrator.

THE SOLUTION

The purpose of literacy intervention is to serve students who struggle. It is not a class that can or should be filled with students who do not qualify based on assessment. Students do not always take assessments as seriously as we would like. However, anecdotal data is not reason enough to remove a student from intervention or to place a student into intervention.

> *"Literacy intervention is a data-driven reform; we must have concrete data to determine correct placement of students."*

Literacy intervention is a data-driven reform; we must have concrete data to determine correct placement of students. In addition, we do not want intervention classes to become dumping grounds for students with behavior issues.

KEYS TO SUCCESS

- Develop a data-driven procedure that everyone will follow for determining if a student is mistakenly placed in intervention or is in need of intervention.
- Do not leave data collection to the literacy coach, literacy team, or site administrator. Give teachers the responsibility for compiling data to support their contentions that a student is mistakenly placed.
- The same data-driven procedure can also be used for students who enroll after the beginning of the school year.

THE WORKSHEET

Use Worksheet 2.6 if you suspect that a student has been mistakenly placed in intervention or, conversely, is in need of intervention. This worksheet can also be used for students who enroll after the school year begins and for students in grade-level classes who might be intervention candidates.

Worksheet 2.6 *Placement Criteria*

Student name _____ Current placement: Core _____ Strategic _____ Intensive _____

Evidence	Meets or exceeds exit criteria	Does not meet exit criteria	Placement based on evidence	Placement recommendation based on data
Original placement data (collected by teacher)				
Formative assessment data (collected by teacher)				
Summative assessment data (collected by teacher)				
Most recent standardized test data (collected by teacher)				
Grades in content-area subjects (collected by teacher)				
Readministration of placement measures (administered by School-Site Literacy Intervention Team, literacy coach, or site administrator)				

Phase 2

Exit Criteria

THE CHALLENGE

Students have completed a semester or a year of literacy instruction. Teachers and parents are clamoring to move students back to the core classes. The latest standardized test scores indicate that intervention students have made growth but are still significantly below grade-level or are approaching the strategic level. An argument is made for exposure to core content. The original state/district mandate called for one or two years of intervention. Time is up. Students cannot receive duplicate credit for a class they have already taken. How does the School-Site Literacy Intervention Team decide if a student is ready to exit the intervention class?

THE SOLUTION

We must first recognize that not all intervention students will progress at the same rate. Intervention is not necessarily a one-day, one-lesson instructional method. Intervention means that it is necessary to assess students regularly, adjust instruction based on the assessment, and teach. We must also take the skill of the teacher into consideration. Is the teacher instructing the designated curriculum or strategies with fidelity? Has the student been absent or has an untrained substitute teacher been teaching the class? Does the student require more time to internalize instruction? All these questions must be weighed when deciding if a student should exit literacy intervention.

"Intervention means that it is necessary to assess students regularly, adjust instruction based on the assessment, and teach ... The ultimate goal is to bring a student as close to grade-level performance as possible."

The School-Site Literacy Intervention Team takes on the role of reviewing the evidence and making a decision for the placement of a student. If the team decides that a student would benefit from additional time, then the placement criteria is revisited and the student remains in literacy intervention. If the team determines that a student would benefit from exiting the intervention, the student is placed into a strategic class and/or grade-level instruction and monitored to determine progress. The ultimate goal is to bring a student as close to grade-level performance as possible. It does not benefit a student to exit intervention only to fail in the grade-level class.

KEYS TO SUCCESS

- The first indicator is the correct placement of the student. Was the student placed in a class that was moving too fast or too slow?
- The second indicator is teacher skill. Was the curriculum taught with fidelity? Did the teacher monitor student progress and adjust instruction as needed? Is there evidence of student progress?
- How close is the student to achieving at grade-level?
- The School-Site Literacy Intervention Team should collect standardized test data, progress data from the intervention class, and student grades. A review of this data will help the team decide the correct placement of the student. While we do not want students in intervention who do not need it, we also do not want to deny students the opportunity to develop the skills necessary to comprehend grade-level material.
- Consider placing the student who is exiting intense intervention into a strategic intervention class along with the grade-level Language Arts class.
- If possible, place exiting students with grade-level teachers who have either taught intervention or work well with struggling students. This will assist with the transition from intervention to grade-level content.
- Consider the whole child, and carefully weigh the probability of success before exiting the student.

THE WORKSHEET

Use Worksheet 2.7 if you feel that a student is ready to exit intervention. A decision to exit intervention cannot be made lightly.

Phase 2

Worksheet 2.7 *Exit Criteria*

Student name _____   Current placement: Strategic _____ Intensive _____

Evidence	Meets or exceeds exit criteria	Does not meet exit criteria	Placement based on evidence	Placement recommendation based on data
Original placement data (collected by teacher)				
Formative assessment data (collected by teacher)				
Summative assessment data (collected by teacher)				
Most recent standardized test data (collected by teacher)				
Grades in content-area subjects (collected by teacher)				
Readministration of placement measures (administered by School-Site Literacy Intervention Team, literacy coach, or site administrator)				

School-Site Mutual Accountability

THE CHALLENGE

Innovations do not automatically run smoothly. Teachers are finding their way through material that is new to them with students who may not be cooperative. Teachers have needs as well. They may have been appointed to teach literacy intervention and may not agree to teach it a second year. The site administrator is now charged with making sure that the intervention is successful. Teachers are observed and evaluated. As the school year progresses, teachers are less enthusiastic, and it has become difficult to recruit teachers for next year. Often, it is not the content of literacy intervention that poses the problem. Typical teacher concerns may include:

+ The need for more careful placement of homogeneous student groups (i.e., special education, general education, ELLs).
+ Not getting materials on time.
+ Not enough protected instructional time.
+ Too many students in a class.
+ Confirming placement of students (i.e., entry and exit).
+ ELLs Level 1 and Level 2 should be homogeneously grouped for oral language instruction.
+ Special education teachers do not have time to serve their whole caseload if they are teaching intervention all day.
+ Train more teachers for intervention so that special education teachers can support all of them.
+ Use a collaborative model for special education, and articulate that configuration.
+ The pacing plan is unrealistic.
+ Lack of dedicated space to teach.
+ Not enough consistent and/or comprehensive training for all intervention teachers.
+ Student behavior issues.
+ All schools in the district should receive in-class professional development beyond initial training.
+ Awareness sessions are needed for parents and non-intervention teachers to garner more support.

Typical teacher questions/comments may include:
+ "How can we plan, monitor progress, and adjust instruction if we never have time to meet?"
+ "How do we infuse core material into intervention classrooms?"
+ "To whom do we go if we have a question or need help?"

✦ "What is the role of the literacy coach?"
✦ "Can we train substitute teachers so that instruction is not interrupted when we are out of class?"
✦ "I would like to observe other intervention classes."

THE SOLUTION

Certainly we do not live in a perfect world, and not all needs are equally met. Literacy intervention impacts the entire school operation. It is truly a second-order change in that it requires middle schools and high schools to shift from content-centered to student-centered instruction. Pressures are placed on intervention teachers to deliver the content with fidelity; therefore, it is necessary to provide specific supports that enable teachers to

"Training, while crucial to literacy intervention, does not solve all problems. As indicated by teacher concerns ... many infrastructure issues that are supposed to support intervention teachers arise."

do the job. Training, while crucial to literacy intervention, does not solve all problems. As indicated by the teacher concerns previously listed, many infrastructure issues that are supposed to support intervention teachers arise. The Mutual Accountability Worksheet (1.8a.1) introduced in Phase 1 is a mechanism to develop pressures and supports between the district and site administrators; the same process is valid at the school site with supports for teachers. Only through collaboration will literacy intervention thrive and students demonstrate the progress expected.

KEYS TO SUCCESS

- Remember that everyone is new to this process. Success will not happen overnight.
- Since the School-Site Literacy Intervention Team is already invested in the plan, delegate the team to develop a "Mutual Accountability" document that reflects the expectations of the site administrator and the needs of the intervention teachers.
- Begin the discussion with the question, "What will help you to instruct literacy intervention with fidelity?"
- Recognize that all needs cannot be met immediately. However, all needs must be addressed either now or in the future.
- Collaborate and negotiate to develop the best literacy plan for your school.
- Revisit the "Mutual Accountability" document yearly to make changes and refinements.

THE WORKSHEETS

Refer to Worksheet 2.8a.1 as an example of documentation of mutual accountability that is needed at the teacher and site administrator levels. Use Worksheet 2.8a.2 to create a mutual accountability model for your school.

Worksheet 2.8a.1 *Mutual Accountability School-Site Administrators/Teachers*

(sample)

"Accountability must be a reciprocal process. For every increment of performance I demand from you, I have an equal responsibility to provide you with the capacity to meet the expectation. Likewise, for every investment you make in my skill and knowledge, I have a reciprocal responsibility to demonstrate some new increment in performance. This is the principle of 'accountability for capacity' … " (Elmore, 2004)

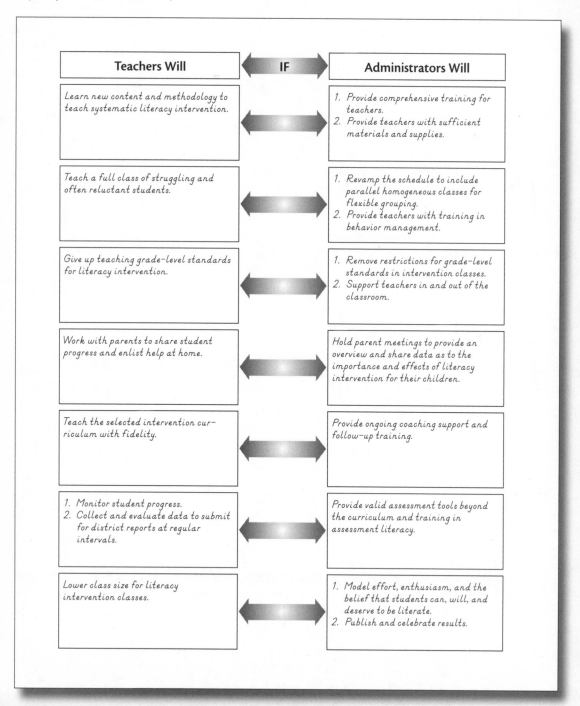

Teachers Will	IF	Administrators Will
Learn new content and methodology to teach systematic literacy intervention.	⟷	1. Provide comprehensive training for teachers. 2. Provide teachers with sufficient materials and supplies.
Teach a full class of struggling and often reluctant students.	⟷	1. Revamp the schedule to include parallel homogeneous classes for flexible grouping. 2. Provide teachers with training in behavior management.
Give up teaching grade-level standards for literacy intervention.	⟷	1. Remove restrictions for grade-level standards in intervention classes. 2. Support teachers in and out of the classroom.
Work with parents to share student progress and enlist help at home.	⟷	Hold parent meetings to provide an overview and share data as to the importance and effects of literacy intervention for their children.
Teach the selected intervention curriculum with fidelity.	⟷	Provide ongoing coaching support and follow-up training.
1. Monitor student progress. 2. Collect and evaluate data to submit for district reports at regular intervals.	⟷	Provide valid assessment tools beyond the curriculum and training in assessment literacy.
Lower class size for literacy intervention classes.	⟷	1. Model effort, enthusiasm, and the belief that students can, will, and deserve to be literate. 2. Publish and celebrate results.

Phase 2

Worksheet 2.8a.2 *Mutual Accountability School-Site Administrators/Teachers*

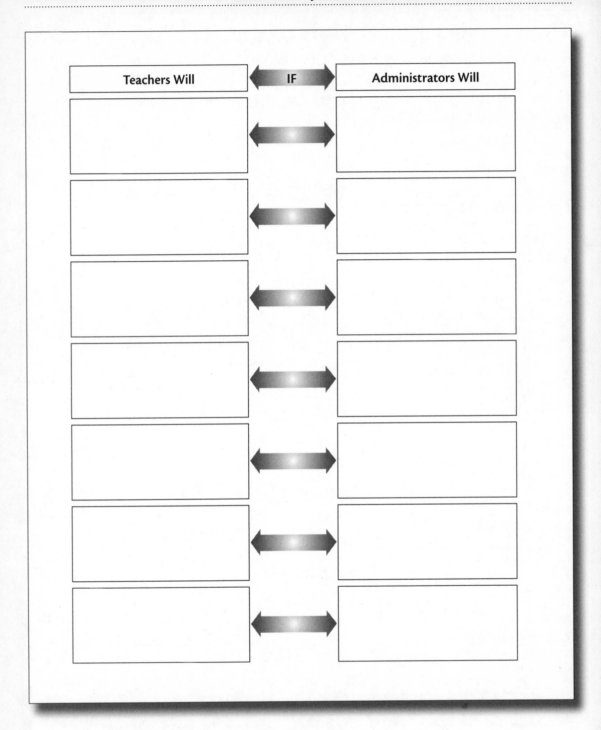

On-Site Professional Development

THE CHALLENGE

Teachers received initial training in the content and methodology of literacy intervention. The school year has started. Upon visiting the classrooms, the administrator notices that literacy instruction looks vastly different from class to class. Each teacher interpreted the training differently, learned what he/she believed was important, and excluded pieces that seemed unimportant or too difficult. The teachers have questions about content and activities because they have never taught reading. It seems that the initial training was a long time ago. If there is no one to ask, teachers either omit an activity or interpret it the best they can. Data gathering and analysis becomes sketchy, at best. The instruction and data analysis lack the coherence necessary to see student growth. In addition, student behavior has become an issue. The classroom management techniques that teachers employed previously do not seem to be working with classes of struggling readers. Teachers struggle through the year and vow not to teach intervention again. How then do we ensure student progress? We know that teaching practice is the factor that most influences student achievement. Teachers constitute the heart of reform (Cohen & Hill, 2000).

THE SOLUTION

Even if initial training is excellent, it is not enough to carry teachers through the actual instructional year. Concepts, research, and instructional activities that seemed clear and essential during the initial training become foggy and difficult. Furthermore, everything changes when we add students to the mix. Students, especially high school students, may be understandably resistant; after all, they have been doing a good job of hiding up to this point. In their analysis of professional development, Snow-Renner and Lauer (2005) report five characteristics that are likely to have a positive effect on instruction:

> *"Ongoing professional development should include follow-up training in literacy strategies, curriculum content and methodology, classroom management, and assessment literacy."*

1. Professional development occurs over a considerable amount of time.
2. Professional development is focused on specific content and/or instructional strategies.
3. Professional development includes collective participation of educators through school or grade-level cohorts.

4. Coherence: everyone receives the same content and message.
5. Professional development includes active learning rather than solely a lecture model.

Snow-Renner and Lauer (2005) assert that teacher learning should occur beyond the initial training. Teachers do not know what they don't understand until they have had the opportunity to implement new instructional practice in a real classroom with real students. Therefore, ongoing professional development is a requirement, not an option.

Ongoing professional development should include follow-up training in literacy strategies, curriculum content and methodology, classroom management, and assessment literacy. This development can be accomplished through training and coaching at the school site. Developing a cadre of literacy coaches whose primary task is assisting teachers with classroom instruction and scheduling follow-up training affords teachers the best chance to refine their practices, resulting in fidelity of instruction and increased student achievement.

KEYS TO SUCCESS

- Base any follow-up training on teacher need and curriculum content.
- Consult the curriculum publisher or literacy consultant concerning difficult curricular areas that might require additional emphasis. They know the obstacles.
- Provide advanced training for literacy coaches. If possible, recruit the coaches from intervention teacher ranks. Coaches are more credible if they have actually taught literacy intervention.
- Protect the coaches' time; they are not pseudo-administrators, test proctors, or deans of discipline. They should not sacrifice valuable in-class time for administrative functions under the "other duties as assigned" category.
- Beware the coach who just wants to be out of the classroom.
- Provide opportunities for teachers to share their practices and their solutions to problems. Sometimes, our best insights come from within.

THE WORKSHEET

Use Worksheet 2.9 as a guide to the type of professional development that can, and should, occur at the school site. Each School-Site Literacy Intervention Team must determine how much professional development its teachers require and how much its school can afford.

Worksheet 2.9 *School-Site Professional Development Checklist*

Type of Development	Dates	Location(s)	Need verified by teachers
Targeted follow-up professional development			
Assessment literacy professional development			
Behavior management professional development			
Coaching			
Observation of other teachers in like settings			
Classroom demonstrations			
Intervention team meetings			
Opportunities to meet, plan, and share			
Regularly scheduled meetings to analyze data and to develop an adjusted instructional plan			
Literacy conferences			
Technology professional development (if applicable)			

Phase 2

Monitoring Progress at the School Site

THE CHALLENGE

A significant amount of money has been invested in materials and teacher training. Schedules have been revamped. Standardized tests may show a small gain, but the gain really doesn't tell you how students are doing. Parallel-scheduling has provided the structure to make sure students are homogeneously grouped, yet teachers are unsure about how or when to move students or adjust instruction. Teachers are moving through the curriculum at a good pace, but are the students moving with them? Teachers are unsure about how to adjust instruction for students who are failing, absent, or new enrollees. Quality training and support has been provided for teachers, but it is still unclear whether the students are making progress. The required assessments are being administered, but nothing is happening as a result.

THE SOLUTION

The concept of assessment literacy outlined by Michael Fullan (2001) was discussed in Phase 1: Initiation. It is now time to put theory into practice at the school site. Literacy intervention requires that we know exactly how our students are performing at every moment. Ongoing or formative assessment has been built into the design of many literacy intervention curricula, but are we using the information to ensure that we are meeting the needs of students? These assessment procedures provide a mechanism to measure student acquisition of literacy skill at short intervals so that instruction may be adjusted according to student need. A skilled literacy intervention teacher not only provides intervention but also engages in prevention by recognizing concepts that are difficult for students, reteaching material based on assessment, and scheduling additional practice in upcoming lessons so that students are successful. Middle school and high school teachers may not be familiar with this type of diagnostic teaching and, therefore, will benefit from instruction in assessment literacy. A consultant, principal, or literacy coach familiar with analyzing and reacting to data can conduct data-analysis meetings.

"Ongoing or formative assessment has been built into the design of many literacy intervention curricula, but are we using the information to ensure that we are meeting the needs of students?"

KEYS TO SUCCESS

- Schedule one School-Site Literacy Intervention Team meeting per month dedicated to data analysis and response.
- Provide data analysis training for teachers. Make sure that the training is specifically based on curricular assessments in use.
- Develop plans for future instruction that will assist students in learning difficult concepts.
- Schedule specific days for students to take missed assessments, to make up work, and to receive extra instruction in difficult concepts.
- Have teachers submit ongoing assessment data to the administrator for accountability purposes.
- Plan quarterly or trimester meetings for teachers to review collected data and to regroup students based on the data results.

THE WORKSHEETS

Use Worksheets 2.10a as a model for identifying, collecting, and responding to intervention data. The worksheet will serve as a reference for developing a more complete process for responding to intervention. Use Worksheet 2.10b to develop a school-site process to monitor progress.

Worksheet 2.10a *Developing a Progress Monitoring Process*

Task	Date	Lead person	Process	Evidence
Set regular dates for weekly/monthly meetings.				
Data collection: • Screening assessment • Formative assessment • Summative assessment • Progress data • Standardized testing				
Data analysis: • Screening assessment • Formative assessment • Summative assessment • Progress data • Standardized testing				
Adjusting instruction based on data.				
Possible movement of students among classes or ready to exit intervention.				
Monitoring students who have exited intervention.				
Addressing the needs of special education students in literacy intervention.				
Addressing the needs of ELLs in literacy intervention.				
Teacher fidelity.				

Worksheet 2.10b *Monthly School-Site Progress Monitoring Checklist*

School _____ Teacher _____ Grade _____

Criteria	Formative assessment	Summative assessment	Progress Monitoring assessment	Notes
Based on data, the number of students achieving mastery in all skills taught who could progress more quickly or be moved to another class.				
Based on data, the number of students who are not mastering concepts or making growth, and who might need to move at a slower pace or be moved to another class.				
Skills that need reinforcement or reteaching as indicated by student data (identify specific skills).				
Response actions.				

Phase 2

Grading Literacy Intervention

THE CHALLENGE

The focus of awarding most grades in middle school and high school rests on student achievement based on grade-level standards or benchmarks. However, students enrolled in literacy intervention are not able to negotiate grade-level standards. The dilemma that faces many districts, schools, and teachers is whether to award grades based on the content the students should be learning at grade-level or the content they are actually learning in the literacy intervention class. This becomes even more complicated if the literacy intervention class supplants the grade-level Language Arts class.

Various opinions will come to the forefront including the issue of fairness. One perspective claims that students in intervention classes are not mastering grade-level concepts, so they should receive grades that reflect that deficiency. Another perspective proposes that students should always be graded on what they are learning. Political pressures are immense, since the grades received could be misinterpreted as achievement of grade-level material. As a consequence, teachers may stray from the literacy intervention curriculum to include and evaluate a student's progress against grade-level benchmarks or award lower grades based on the skill levels of the students.

THE SOLUTION

A student in strategic or intensive intervention is performing below grade-level. Students are enrolled in this class because they cannot access grade-level material, and the only hope is for them to develop the literacy skills necessary to successfully engage in core content. Intervention students may have been receiving failing grades or "mercy" grades that allowed them to barely pass, but mercy grades do not assist in literacy acquisition. We must grade intervention students on the instructional content. If students are learning what we teach them, why would we diminish their achievements by awarding them artificially low grades? Intervention-content grading is easier in middle school than in high school because high school educators are primarily concerned about college credit and credit for graduation. Remember that students who continually fail are in danger of dropping out or not passing high school exit

"We must grade intervention students on the instructional content. If students are learning what we teach them, why would we diminish their achievements by awarding them artificially low grades [based on grade-level material]?"

exams. Not only do we want to make sure our students graduate from high school, we want them to have choices for college or vocational education. In some instances, districts have renamed or in some way designated that literacy intervention classes do not meet grade-level or college requirements, but students are still awarded grades based on mastery of content taught.

Grading has always been the domain of the individual teacher. However, students' progress in intervention must be carefully monitored if we are to make informed instructional decisions. Therefore, it is important for the School-Site Literacy Intervention Team to develop a common grading criteria primarily based on curriculum content. This data will be used to inform the team of student progress, the next year's placements for students, and exit criteria.

KEYS TO SUCCESS

- Be realistic. Ensure that everyone involved understands that without literacy intervention, students may have no hope of graduation, much less college or vocational education.
- Keep in mind that the ultimate goal of intense and strategic literacy intervention is to bring students within striking range of grade-level material as quickly as possible, with mastery.
- Ensure that the School-Site Literacy Intervention Team develops a common grading criterion that includes content taught as well as additional criteria (e.g., intervention assessments, completed assignments, homework, participation, effort) determined by the team.
- Remember that the literacy intervention class is designated as an elective for strategic classes and complements grade-level instruction.
- Remember that the intense intervention class replaces the grade-level class and one elective. The classes are blocked to allow time for intensive instruction, and the student receives one grade for both classes based on content taught.
- If the computer requires a grade for each period, then grade each period identically. For example, a literacy intervention block entitled "English 9/Literacy for Success" would receive two identical grades. (Sometimes, we just have to feed the computer what it wants.)
- Note that students must earn a grade of at least 80 percent to indicate mastery of the content being taught. If that is not the case, it is important to understand why the grade is lower. Is the student absence rate high? Is the teacher grading on the literacy intervention content? Does the student require additional instruction? All of these factors must be considered if we are basing instruction on student need.

THE WORKSHEET

Use Worksheet 2.11 to develop a common district/school grading policy for strategic and/or intensive students enrolled in literacy intervention. Sample grading items are included for review and discussion. Blank spaces are provided to develop a more detailed grading policy unique to your district/school.

Phase 2

Worksheet 2.11 *Grading Criteria Checklist*

Evaluation Items	Evidence	Percent of grade or point totals

Sample curricular assessments:
▪ *Ongoing assessments*
  ✦ *Formal*
  ✦ *Informal*
▪ *Summative assessments*		

Classwork: ▪ *Completed assignments* ▪ *Selected graded assignments* ▪ *Group or individual projects*		
Homework: ▪ *Completed homework* ▪ *Selected graded homework assignments* ▪ *Selected assignments*		
Non-graded evaluations: ▪ *Participation* ▪ *Citizenship* ▪ *Attendance* ▪ *Student self-evaluation*		

Continuance

PHASE 3: *Continuance*

Continuance is the third phase in the change process (Fullan, 2001). The term refers to the institutionalization of an innovation or reform; in this case, literacy intervention. The infrastructure, policies, and mutual accountability developed in the initiation and implementation phases will determine whether system-wide literacy intervention is sustained beyond the initial implementation. Careful planning up to this stage helps the innovation survive budget cuts, change in personnel, and school board changes. Of course, it is hoped that the need for intervention will decrease over time, but it will not disappear. Some students will always be in need of our help; thus, the continuance phase is the ongoing path of refinement and improvement. It does not mean that we can heave a sigh of relief and move on to the next project; sustainability requires constant vigilance.

The Role of Administration in Continuance

THE CHALLENGE

The role of administration has already been discussed in the implementation phase. However, the continuance phase of literacy implementation presents additional challenges for school and district administrations. New mandates, adoptions, and innovations do not cease simply because a literacy intervention has been chosen and implemented. Administrators continually have new mandates to implement, and there are not enough hours in the day to take care of everything.

The major challenge for administration in this phase of literacy intervention is to continue overt support. With new crises and mandates, this is not an easy task. As implementation moves toward continuance, it is easy to assume that literacy intervention does not need attention. Once attention is diverted, the passion and effort that characterized the initiation and implementation phases may drift. Educators come and go, and the gains made previously begin to diminish.

THE SOLUTION

This is the time when all the previous structures that have been put into place show their real value. The district and school-site literacy teams must remain in place and remain dedicated to literacy intervention. The schedule of meetings and data collection must continue. Therefore, it is up to the administration to keep the effort alive, to continue to pressure and support, and to recruit new intervention teachers to assist students in need. Intervention teachers will take their cues from the actions or inactions of the school administrator.

" … it is up to the administration to keep the effort alive, to continue to pressure and support, and to recruit new intervention teachers to assist students in need."

KEYS TO SUCCESS

- Keep the School-Site Literacy Intervention Team intact, and continue to meet regularly.
- If members of the School-Site Literacy Intervention Team leave the school or district, replace them immediately with equally qualified people.
- Understand that the student gains achieved will not continue without support.
- Continue to visit classrooms and celebrate teacher and student success.

- Do not siphon resources from literacy intervention. This may be interpreted as a lack of interest by implementers, which will cause instruction to suffer.
- Continue to build a culture of literacy at the school site.
- Continue to schedule professional development for literacy teachers.

THE WORKSHEET

Worksheet 3.1 provides a format for keeping track of ongoing implementation needs that require attention every year. Continued use of this worksheet will serve as a reminder and a record to ensure that literacy intervention is successfully sustained.

Worksheet 3.1 *Literacy Intervention Continuance Checklist*

Task	Person responsible	Notes
District Literacy Intervention Committee		
1. Secure literacy intervention funding.		
2. Schedule ongoing administrator training.		
3. Schedule school-site visits for observation.		
4. Schedule yearly data review with administrators.		
5. Schedule yearly review and approval of school-site plans.		
6. Schedule yearly review of district literacy plan.		
7. Review student progress goals.		
8. Prepare yearly Board Report on student progress.		
9. Schedule Performance Plan meetings with administrators.		
10. Order/reorder materials.		
11. Schedule ongoing administrator training.		
School-Site Administrator		
1. Schedule classroom visits and evaluations.		
2. Update and submit school-site plan based on student data.		
3. Schedule reviews of student progress data.		
4. Select literacy intervention coaches.		
5. Prepare student progress reports for the district, staff, and parents.		
6. Schedule Performance Plan meetings with teachers.		
7. Submit orders for materials to the district committee.		
8. Schedule necessary training for teachers.		

Creating a Culture of Literacy

THE CHALLENGE

Awareness sessions are discussed in the implementation phase. Once completed, it may seem that everyone understands and is ready to move ahead. However, without an embedded culture of literacy at the school, the intervention department can become separate from the school community as a whole. Other staff members may look upon the intervention as "those teachers with those kids." Everyone at the school site knows who the intervention students are. Unless literacy is a whole-school focus, intervention students and teachers may become stigmatized. This informal branding, coupled with new innovations that require attention, can demote literacy intervention to an innovation in name only.

THE SOLUTION

The infrastructure that has been developed must encompass more than just the literacy intervention team. Awareness, while critical in the beginning stages, is not enough to sustain the belief that literacy intervention is necessary and beneficial to the entire school community. Gladwell (2000, p. 173) writes: "If you want … to bring about fundamental change in people's belief and behavior, and change that would persist as an example to others, you need to create a community around them, where these new beliefs could be practiced, expressed, and nurtured." Developing a school culture of literacy serves to build that community. It is only during the later stages of the implementation phase and during the continuation phase that we begin to notice that strategies used in intervention have filtered into grade-level classes. It is at that point that the entire faculty begins to see the benefit of literacy instruction for all students.

> *"Awareness, while critical in the beginning stages, is not enough to sustain the belief that literacy intervention is necessary and beneficial to the entire school community."*

Lein, Johnson, and Ragland (1997) identified seven characteristics of successful schools in Texas that we can certainly apply to a well-planned, quality literacy intervention effort:

1. A strong focus on ensuring the academic success of each student. The schools established clear, measurable goals that focused on student achievement.
2. The schools exhibited a "no excuses" attitude toward student achievement. Educators believed they could succeed with any student.

3. The schools were willing to experiment with new instructional strategies to ensure student success.

4. The schools involved everyone—including staff, students, and parents—who could help them attain their goals.

5. The schools created an environment in which students, teachers, parents, support staff, and administrators functioned more as a family that focused on improving student achievement.

6. The schools exhibited an open, honest, and trusting approach to collaboration among school personnel.

7. A passion for continuous improvement, professional growth, and learning pervaded the school climate.

The school staff members pushed themselves to refine their practices, and they celebrated their successes. The themes articulated by Lein et al. embody the tenets of continuance for literacy intervention.

KEYS TO SUCCESS

- Continue to conduct scheduled formal and informal classroom visits.
- Have intervention teachers share strategies with content teachers that will help struggling readers without sacrificing grade-level content.
- Schedule and continue awareness and progress sessions for teachers, parents, and administrators.
- Share student progress data at whole-staff meetings.
- Continue to meet and plan with the School-Site Literacy Intervention Team to review data and to refine the literacy plan.
- Recruit new intervention teachers.
- Build a high-interest, low-level reading library for intervention students.
- Create a Literacy Intervention Department within the school.
- Allow both content and intervention teachers to visit each other's classes to better understand the expectations in each class.
- Share data reports with students and parents.
- Continue to celebrate successes with yearly awards ceremonies.
- Solicit information from content teachers as to the performance of intervention students.
- Use grade-level content material to read aloud in intervention classrooms.

THE WORKSHEET

Worksheet 3.2 is designed to be used during the first year of intervention implementation and every year thereafter. Creating a culture of literacy is a long-term project; continued use of this worksheet will serve as a constant reminder that we must be vigilant for all students to succeed.

Worksheet 3.2 *Creating a Culture of Literacy Checklist*

Task	Date accomplished or ongoing	Notes
Schedule formal and informal classroom visits.		
Provide opportunities for literacy intervention teachers to share strategies with content teachers.		
Schedule parent meetings and prepare reports for distribution to parents.		
Hold an annual recognition ceremony for intervention students.		
Recruit teachers who are willing and able to teach intervention.		
Share data reports with students, teachers, and parents.		
Schedule regular meeting times with intervention teachers.		
Meet with intervention teachers to review the school-site plan.		
Meet with intervention teachers to review student progress and to adjust teaching plans.		
Schedule training and observations for intervention teachers.		
Build a high-interest, low-level reading library for intervention students.		
Order supplies for intervention classes.		
Create a Literacy Intervention Department within the school.		
Schedule meetings with literacy coaches.		

Phase 3

Parents

THE CHALLENGE

Parents are an important part of any school community. Many parents are shocked when informed that their child requires literacy intervention. Struggling readers who are not identified as special education do an excellent job of hiding the fact that they cannot negotiate grade-level texts. The parents may be aware of low grades, low test scores, and behavior issues, but they may have been told that their child is too social, lacks motivation, and is disruptive in class. This is not a criticism of educators; for many years, we did not analyze why middle school and high school students were performing below grade-level. Therefore—and rightfully so—some parents are angry and frightened for their child. They want their child to graduate from high school but may be reluctant to understand that in order to do so, their child must acquire advanced literacy skills. They want what is best for their child. Parents have been notified of the need for intervention and may also have attended the awareness session, but that is not enough if we hope to foster parent support.

THE SOLUTION

Parents are a crucial part of literacy intervention. If the school develops a true culture of literacy, participation of all stakeholders is necessary. As implementation moves toward continuance, teachers and administrators need parents more than ever. Parents can be the public-relations vehicles for literacy intervention. They can help their own child, as well as other parents and children, to understand that difficulty with reading is not shameful. Needing help does not mean that their child is less intelligent than others. Fullan (2003, p. 44) describes the need for parent involvement in learning communities: "By contrast, professional learning communities not only build confidence and competence but they also make teachers and principals realize that they can't go the distance alone. To these educators, inevitably, I would say, 'Begin to reach out to and become more responsive to parent involvement and community development.'" Mobilize your parent community; let them help you close the achievement gap.

> "As implementation moves toward continuance, teachers and administrators need parents more than ever. They can help their child … understand that difficulty with reading is not shameful."

KEYS TO SUCCESS

- Invite parents to observe classroom instruction.
- Share student progress at parent organization meetings.
- Develop a parent newsletter to inform them of literacy events.
- Suggest that the parent organization form a Literacy Booster Club to raise money for supplies and library books.
- Allow intervention parents to share in their child's success at parent organization meetings.
- Develop student-led parent conferences during which students explain the content of their class and their progress based on data.
- Invite parents to annual awards ceremonies for their children. (It may be the first time this group of parents has come to school for a positive reason!)
- Send periodic progress reports to parents, including movement based on data.
- Develop family literacy classes after school.

THE WORKSHEET

Worksheet 3.3 outlines an outreach process. The worksheet is by no means all-encompassing, but it provides suggestions to help schools solicit parental involvement.

Phase 3

Worksheet 3.3 *Parent/Guardian Involvement Checklist*

(The word *parent* in this worksheet is defined as a parent or legal guardian.)

Task	Date completed or ongoing	Person responsible	Notes
Notify parents that their children will be enrolled in literacy intervention classes.			
Hold an awareness session for parents to attend at the beginning of every school year.			
Select parents to participate in the School-Site Literacy Intervention Team.			
Invite parents to visit literacy intervention classrooms during instruction.			
Instruct parents in strategies they can use at home to assist their children.			
Ensure that PTA meetings include literacy intervention progress reports every quarter.			
Ask parents to talk about the changes in their child's reading behavior at home.			
Ask the PTA to raise funds for in-class libraries for literacy intervention classes.			
Plan an end-of-year literacy celebration that will include students, teachers, administrators, parents/guardians, and the students' families.			

The Role of the Consultant

THE CHALLENGE

Educational consultants can either be assets or detriments to the implementation and sustainability of literacy intervention. Not all consultants are created equally; literacy is not a "one-size-fits-all" proposition. Literacy is a specific area of expertise, and it requires significant knowledge and experience. Implementation and sustainability of a reform initiative also requires successful experience. Lack of knowledge on the part of a district or a school's administrators can result in spending vast amounts of money on consulting fees without reaping proportionate rewards.

THE SOLUTION

In the initial stages, an informed literacy consultant with validated experience can help the district and school walk through planning and implementation of literacy intervention. The consultant can act as literacy coach, facilitate meetings, visit classrooms, demonstrate lessons, teach strategy, and build a good implementation and continuance plan. The consultant's role diminishes as internal expertise is developed at the school site. The title "Literacy Consultant" does not necessarily mean experience with the chosen literacy curriculum, strategies, types of student, or structural configurations that exist in every district or school.

"The title 'Literacy Consultant' does not necessarily mean experience with the chosen literacy curriculum, strategies, types of student, or structural configurations that exist in every district or school."

You must ensure that there is alignment between the expertise of the literacy consultant and the configuration and curriculum of your district or school.

KEYS TO SUCCESS

- Solicit recommendations for consultants from districts that are implementing a similar literacy intervention.
- Check with the publisher of your district's or school's chosen literacy intervention curriculum for experienced consultants.
- Interview consultants, and check their references.
- Articulate the tasks that you want the consultant to perform.

Phase 3

- Check the consultant's availability for one to two years.
- While interviewing consultant candidates, consider these points:
  - ✦ Does the consultant have experience in literacy instruction, implementation planning, or both?
  - ✦ Does the consultant have specific experience with the instructional curriculum and strategies being utilized?
  - ✦ Are the consultant's fees commensurate with firms providing like services?
  - ✦ Does the consultant have experience working with teachers, administrators, students, and parents?
  - ✦ What is the consultant's view on reading instruction for middle school or high school students?

THE WORKSHEET

Worksheet 3.4 is designed to assist schools in selecting an intervention consultant who will maximize the literacy effort. You are looking for the right person for the right job.

Worksheet 3.4 *Choosing a Literacy Intervention Consultant*

Consultant candidate _____

Interview preparation tasks	Task completion date	Notes
Research consultant groups.		
Convene an interview panel that includes administrators and teachers.		
Schedule interviews.		

Interview points	Rate on scale 1–5	Interviewer	Date of interview	Notes
Does the candidate have expertise in explicit, systemic instruction for literacy intervention?				
Are the candidate's views of literacy instruction in line with current reading research?				
Does the candidate have expertise in the literacy intervention curriculum chosen by the district/school?				
Does the candidate have experience in student grouping, behavior management, and blended classes?				
Does the candidate have experience working with teachers, administrators, and parents?				
Can the candidate's expertise be confirmed through references?				
Result of review of consultant's plan?				
Result of review of consultant's fees?				
Number of days per week/month the consultant will be able to visit the school site?				

Phase 3

Planning for the Future

THE CHALLENGE

The purpose of initiating, implementing, and sustaining literacy intervention is to help struggling readers realize their potential and to enable them to participate in an increasingly complex world. However, it is difficult to plan for a future in which budgets, educational agendas, students, and educators shift with the breeze. We prepare knowing that our plans may be undone with the next district administration. Sometimes, the effort feels futile.

THE SOLUTION

The plans we develop are about children. Although the structures outlined in this book have focused primarily on the actions of adults, we must remember that we enact them to assist children. We will always have children who are in need of literacy intervention. We expect, through our efforts, that the need for intervention will decrease. However, the structures and cultures developed in this process will ensure that the middle school and high school models will have changed from content-centered to student-centered. The development of a long-term plan—with timelines—improves the odds that literacy intervention will become a permanent aspect of middle school- and high school-level educational processes.

"We will always have children who are in need of literacy intervention. We expect, through our efforts, that the need for intervention will decrease."

KEYS TO SUCCESS

- Develop a timeline that spans five to eight years.
- Set up a yearly review of the plan, and adjust the goals according to student progress data.
- Designate a person who will be responsible for each aspect of the plan. (The people may change, but the need for carrying out the tasks will not.)

THE WORKSHEET

Refer to the series of tables in Worksheet 3.5 to itemize the logistic aspects of attending to literacy intervention over a five-year period. (Each district/school should develop a five-year timeline specific to their domain because the time frames and tasks will be unique to each situation.)

Worksheet 3.5 *Long-Range Implementation Plans*

(samples)

Sample Year 0: School Year: 2006–2007   Initiation for grades 6–12

Time frame	Task	Explanation
September–October 2006	Select a Literacy Intervention Coordinator and District Literacy Intervention Committee members.	Candidates are interviewed and selected. Literacy intervention plan is developed.
October–December 2006	Select literacy intervention curriculum.	Curriculum materials for both strategic and intensive intervention levels are reviewed and selected.
January 2007–March 2007	Schedule awareness sessions.	Awareness sessions are conducted for administrators, teachers, staff, and parents.
May 2007–July 2007	Select and train teachers.	Teachers for strategic and intensive literacy intervention are selected and receive initial training.
	Identify assessment(s) to determine progress.	Assessment(s) beyond the curriculum are identified and purchased to determine student progress on an independent measure.
March–June 2007	Assess and identify intervention students.	Students are assessed, and assessment data is reviewed to determine possible numbers of strategic-level and intensive-level students and classes.
	Plan the schedules.	Master schedules are redesigned to incorporate parallel schedules for homogeneous and flexible student groupings.
	Order the materials.	Materials are ordered for all classes.
April–July 2007	Set up administrator training.	Administrators participate in training on the components of literacy intervention and implementation plans.

Phase 3

Worksheet 3.5 *Long-Range Implementation Plans*

(samples)

Sample Year 1: School Year: 2007–2008 Implementation for grades 6–12

Time Frame	Task	Explanation
September–October 2007	Schedule awareness sessions.	Awareness sessions are held to inform parents and staff.
October 2007	Complete student selection and placement.	Late enrollees are assessed and placed into classes.
	Develop a School-Site Literacy Intervention Team.	The School-Site Literacy Intervention Team is convened to articulate the literacy intervention plan at the school site.
September 2007–June 2008	Monitor student progress.	Students are pretested to determine baseline data and posttested at regular intervals to determine progress. During this time, teachers meet monthly to analyze student data and regroup students, if necessary.
	Select and train literacy coaches.	Literacy coaches are chosen from the pool of intervention teachers. They are provided with advanced professional development in research, content, methodology, and implementation as well as training in working with adults.
October 2007–June 2008	Schedule follow-up instruction for teachers.	Depending on need, teachers receive three follow-up sessions on intervention content and strategy.
March 2008	Plan for summer training.	Summer 2008 training is planned and booked for designated teachers, administrators, and new hires. Follow-up training is planned for administrators.
March–June 2008	Assess and identify intervention students.	Students are assessed, and assessment data is reviewed to determine the possible numbers of strategic-level and intensive-level students and classes for the upcoming school year.
	Plan the schedules.	Master schedules are redesigned to incorporate parallel schedules for homogeneous and flexible student groupings.
	Order materials.	New materials and reorders of student materials are processed as needed.
April–June 2008	Select and assess students for school year 2008–2009.	Students who meet the criteria for intervention are assessed for placement (i.e., strategic and intensive levels).
June 2008	Have the District Literacy Intervention Committee review student progress data.	The District Literacy Intervention Committee reviews and analyzes student data and reports results to the board of education.
	Schedule progress sessions.	Progress sessions are held at each school site for parents, students, and teachers.
June–October 2008	Select and train intervention teachers.	New teachers are selected and trained as needed.

Worksheet 3.5 *Long-Range Implementation Plans*

(samples)

Sample Year 2: School Year: 2008–2009 — Implementation for grades 6–12

Time frame	Task	Explanation
September 2008	Complete student Selection and placement process.	Late enrollees are assessed and placed into strategic or intensive classes.
September–October 2008	Schedule awareness sessions.	Awareness sessions are conducted to inform parents and staff.
	Schedule a meeting of the School-Site Literacy Intervention Team.	The School-Site Literacy Intervention Team is convened to review the school-site plan, review student data, develop yearly goals, and monitor student progress.
September 2008–June 2009	Monitor student progress.	Students are pretested to determine baseline data and posttested at regular intervals to determine progress. During this time, teachers meet monthly to analyze student data and regroup students, if necessary.
	Select and train literacy coaches.	Literacy coaches are chosen from the pool of intervention teachers. They are provided with advanced professional development in research, content, methodology, and implementation as well as training in working with adults.
October 2008–June 2009	Schedule follow-up instruction for teachers.	Depending on need, teachers receive three follow-up sessions on curriculum content and strategy.
March 2009	Plan for summer training.	Summer 2009 training is planned and booked for designated teachers, administrators, and new hires. Follow-up training is planned for administrators.
March–June 2009	Assess and identify intervention students.	Students are assessed, and assessment data is reviewed to determine the possible numbers of strategic-level and intensive-level students and classes for the upcoming school year.
	Plan the schedules.	Master schedules are redesigned to incorporate parallel schedules for homogeneous and flexible student groupings.
	Order materials.	New materials and reorders of student materials are processed as needed.
April–June 2009	Select and assess students for school year 2009–2010.	Students who meet the criteria for intervention are assessed for placement (i.e., strategic and intensive levels).
June 2009	Have the District Literacy Intervention Committee review student progress data.	The District Literacy Intervention Committee reviews and analyzes student data and reports results to the board of education.
	Schedule progress sessions.	Progress sessions are held at each school site for parents, students, and teachers.
June–October 2009	Select and train intervention teachers.	New teachers are selected and trained as needed.

Worksheet 3.5 *Long-Range Implementation Plans*

....

(samples)

Sample Year 3: School Year: 2009–2010   Implementation for grades 6–12

Time frame	Task	Explanation
September 2009	Complete student selection and placement.	Late enrollees are assessed and placed into classes.
September–October 2009	Schedule awareness sessions.	Awareness sessions are held to inform parents and staff.
September–October 2009	Schedule a meeting for the School-Site Literacy Intervention Team.	The School-Site Literacy Intervention Team is convened to review the site plan, review student data, develop yearly goals, and monitor student progress.
September 2009–June 2010	Monitor student progress.	Students are pretested to determine baseline data and posttested at regular intervals to determine progress. During this time, teachers meet monthly to analyze student data and regroup students, if necessary.
September 2009–June 2010	Select and train literacy coaches.	Literacy coaches are chosen from the pool of intervention teachers. They are provided with advanced professional development in research, content, methodology, and implementation as well as training in working with adults.
October 2009–June 2010	Schedule follow-up instruction for teachers.	Depending on need, teachers receive three follow-up sessions on intervention content and strategy.
March 2010	Plan for summer training.	Summer 2010 training is planned and booked for designated teachers, administrators, and new hires. Follow-up training is planned for administrators.
March–June 2010	Assess and identify intervention students.	Students are assessed, and assessment data is reviewed to determine the possible numbers of strategic-level and intensive-level students and classes for the upcoming school year.
March–June 2010	Plan the schedules.	Master schedules are redesigned to incorporate parallel schedules for homogeneous and flexible student groupings.
April–June 2010	Order materials.	New materials and reorders of student materials are processed as needed.
April–June 2010	Select and assess students for school year 2010–2011.	Students who meet the criteria for intervention are assessed for placement (i.e., strategic and intensive levels).
June 2010	Have the District Literacy Intervention Committee review student progress data.	The District Literacy Intervention Committee reviews and analyzes student data and reports results to the board of education.
June 2010	Schedule progress sessions.	Progress sessions are held at each school site for parents, students, and teachers.
June–October 2010	Select and train intervention teachers.	New teachers are selected and trained as needed.

Worksheet 3.5 *Long-Range Implementation Plans*

(samples)

Sample Year 4: School Year: 2010–2011   Implementation for grades 6–12

Time frame	Task	Explanation
September 2010	Complete student selection and placement.	Late enrollees are assessed and placed into classes.
	Schedule a meeting of the School-Site Literacy Intervention Team.	The School-Site Literacy Intervention Team is convened to review the school-site plan, review student data, develop yearly goals, and monitor student progress.
September–October 2010	Schedule awareness sessions.	Awareness sessions are held to inform parents and staff.
September 2010– June 2011	Monitor student progress.	Students are pretested to determine baseline data and posttested at regular intervals to determine progress. During this time, teachers meet monthly to analyze student data and regroup students, if necessary.
	Select and train literacy coaches.	Literacy coaches are chosen from the pool of intervention teachers. They are provided with advanced professional development in research, content, methodology, and implementation as well as training in working with adults.
October 2010–June 2011	Schedule follow-up instruction for teachers.	Depending on need, teachers receive three follow-up sessions on curriculum content and strategy.
March 2011	Plan for summer training.	Summer 2011 training is planned and booked for designated teachers, administrators, and new hires. Follow-up training is planned for administrators.
March–June 2011	Assess and identify intervention students.	Students are assessed, and assessment data is reviewed to determine the possible numbers of strategic-level and intensive-level students and classes for the upcoming school year.
	Plan the schedules.	Master schedules are redesigned to incorporate parallel schedules for homogeneous and flexible student groupings.
	Order materials.	New materials and reorders of student materials are processed as needed.
April–June 2011	Select and assess students for school year 2011–2012.	Students who meet the criteria for intervention are assessed for placement (i.e., strategic and intensive levels).
June 2011	Have the District Literacy Intervention Committee review student progress data.	The District Literacy Intervention Committee reviews and analyzes student data and reports results to the board of education.
	Schedule progress sessions.	Progress sessions are held at each school site for parents, students, and teachers.
June–October 2011	Select and train intervention teachers.	New teachers are selected and trained as needed.

Phase 3

Parting Words

Articulation

THE CHALLENGE

At the risk of being overly redundant, the following challenges may continue to plague schools attempting to implement literacy intervention without an articulated, comprehensive plan. Students are not making the progress expected, and instruction is different from room to room. Teachers are supplementing the literacy intervention with extraneous materials. The district and site administration have discussed the need to teach literacy with fidelity, but it seems that literacy intervention is occurring in name only. If students are supposed to be receiving intense or strategic instruction, it must be worth the time taken from other subjects. We cannot afford to waste our students' time.

THE SOLUTION

Marzano, Waters, and McNulty (2005) delineated first-order change (i.e., tweaking what is already being done) and second-order change (i.e., a dramatic departure from the norm). As previously discussed, literacy intervention at the middle school and high school levels is considered second-order change. Marzano et al. go on to cite a difficulty of second-order change: "The common human response is to address virtually all problems as though they were first-order change issues. It makes sense that we would tend to approach new problems from the perspective of our experiences—as issues that can be solved using our previous repertoire of solutions" (p. 67).

"If the plan, process, content, and methodology for literacy intervention are not clearly articulated for teachers, it is natural for them to drift from the original design."

If the plan, process, content, and methodology for literacy intervention are not clearly articulated for teachers, it is natural for them to drift from the original design. Again, middle school and high school teachers may not have a background in reading instruction; consequently, their learning curve is as high as the students'. We must engage in mutual accountability to help teachers realize student potential. Therefore, both the design and the plan of the intervention class must be structured and articulated if we expect teachers to perform the tasks assigned to them.

KEYS TO SUCCESS

- Don't keep the plan to yourself—articulate it for all stakeholders.
- Be transparent in all expectations from stakeholders.
- Ensure that intensive and strategic literacy intervention curricula contain specific content, sequence, and methodology. The curricula must be followed as designed to obtain results.
- Consider these questions:
  - ◆ If the time scheduled exceeds the class time needed to complete a lesson or unit, are there designated activities for the rest of the class period? Are all teachers following the same plan for excess time?
  - ◆ If a class period is too short for delivery of content, is there a common design for the completion of the instruction?
  - ◆ Does the pacing plan include time for reteaching, make-up, and review of content? What does this instruction look like, and when does it occur?
  - ◆ Does the pacing plan take student differences into consideration?
  - ◆ If students receive a strategic reading class, what is the content and instructional methodology? What materials are used?
  - ◆ Do intervention teachers have input for the design of the strategic literacy class?
  - ◆ Do all teachers have specific guidelines for the content of their strategic reading class?
  - ◆ Is the content of the strategic reading class based on assessed student need? What assessments are used? How is progress measured?

THE WORKSHEET

Use Worksheet 4.1 as a vehicle for literacy teams to articulate a common understanding about the implications and specifics of literacy intervention. The worksheet contains the types of questions and concerns often voiced by teachers. If these items are addressed, everyone has a clear picture of expectations.

Worksheet 4.1 *Literacy Intervention Articulation Checklist*

Task or question	Person responsible	Due date	Notes
Document entry criteria for strategic and intensive intervention students.			
Document exit criteria for strategic and intensive intervention students.			
Who will teach intervention?			
Develop a training schedule and topics for intervention teachers.			
Document strategic intervention class size and composition.			
Document intensive intervention class size and composition.			
Create strategic intervention class schedules.			
Create intensive intervention class schedules.			
Establish duration of strategic intervention instruction within a school day.			
Establish duration of intensive intervention instruction within a school day.			
How is the strategic intervention class structured in terms of instruction, length of time, and materials?			
How is the intensive intervention class structured in terms of instruction, length of time, and materials?			
What data will be collected and when?			
Document a grading policy.			
Document a homework policy.			
Create a form of parental notification of children's placement and progress.			
At what point(s) in the curriculum will make-up work/reteaching/retesting occur?			
Establish pacing parameters based on data.			
When and how will data be analyzed?			
How is class material ordered and distributed?			

Creating the Literacy Intervention Handbook

THE CHALLENGE

Education resides in a sea of memoranda. It seems that every time there is a change, new idea, or reinforcement, everyone gets the memo. Unfortunately, many of those memos find their way to the pile we never look at and eventually become scrap paper. No one can remember which memo said what or even remember where the memo is. The solution? Everyone makes it up as they go along. You have gone to all the trouble of articulating a comprehensive plan for literacy intervention; it would be a shame if your plan weren't used.

THE SOLUTION

My final suggestion for planning literacy intervention is to develop a simple, clearly articulated handbook that contains all infrastructural procedures and frequently asked questions. It is an important resource for district administrators, site administrators, counselors, coaches, and teachers. A handbook also becomes part of the pressures and supports to sustain literacy intervention. It is a pressure because everyone has the same guidelines, and everyone can be held accountable for adhering to them. It is a support because stakeholders can access immediate answers to their questions. A handbook is not a static document; along with the intervention plan, it is reviewed and revised yearly.

"In addition to a district-level handbook, each school site should develop a plan and a handbook that articulates how district mandates will be applied at the school."

The following suggestions for handbook content are general and may not pertain to all districts. The objective is to anticipate the everyday questions and concerns that will face teachers and site administrators. Solicit feedback from all stakeholders before developing a handbook. In addition to a district-level handbook, each school site should develop a plan and a handbook that articulates how district mandates will be applied at the school.

Suggested Sections for a Literacy Intervention Handbook

- Mission statement
- Student goals (Year 1)
- Members and contact information:
    - District Literacy Intervention Committee
    - School-Site Literacy Intervention Team
    - Literacy intervention coach(es)
- Curricula and strategies:
    - Strategic level
    - Intensive level
- Student placement:
    - Who is eligible, and how will students be identified?
        - General education
        - Special education
        - ELLs
        - First screening/second screening
        - Placement measures
        - New students
- Class configuration:
    - Grade-specific (e.g., sixth grade or seventh grade) or grade-blended (e.g., sixth grade and seventh grade)
    - Inclusion of general education, special education, and ELLs
    - How will intervention occur?
        - Within the core class (strategic):
          An additional class period for strategic students
        - In place of core instruction (intensive):
          Two blocked class periods for intensive students
        - Student-to-teacher ratio
- Confirmation of placement (misplaced students)
- Exit criteria
- Who teaches literacy intervention?
    - General education teachers
    - Special education teachers
    - Literacy coaches
- Professional development offerings:
    - District level
    - School-site level
- Instructional day (i.e., what should happen in the classroom):
    - Strategic class
    - Intensive class
    - Collaboration model

- Grading
- Data collection and what do teachers do with it?
  - Ongoing assessment
  - Summative assessment
  - Progress monitoring assessment
  - Standardized assessment
  - Required reports
- Working with parents:
  - Sample letter of notification
  - Awareness sessions
  - Progress reports
  - Guidelines for parents to help their children at home
- Appendix:
  - Guidelines for a collaboration model
  - Sample Weekly Lesson Plans for strategic and intensive classes
  - Pacing plans for strategic and intensive classes
  - Guidelines for report cards
  - Sample student data-reporting forms
  - Sample parent letter in several languages
  - Sample student reports for parents

Bibliography

Berninger, V., & Richards, T. L. (2002). *Brain literacy for educators and psychologists.* San Diego, CA: Elsevier Science (USA).

Biancarosa, G., & Snow, C. (2004). *A vision for action and research in middle and high school literacy: A report to the Carnegie Corporation of New York.* New York: Carnegie Corporation.

Carter, S. C. (2001). *No excuses: Lessons from 21 high-performing, high-poverty schools.* Washington, DC: The Heritage Foundation.

Chall, J. S. (2000). *The academic achievement challenge: What really works in the classroom.* New York: The Guilford Press.

Cohen, D. K., & Hill, H. C. (2000, February). Instructional policy and classroom performance: The mathematics reform in California. *Teachers College Record, 102*(2), 294–393.

Curtis, M. (2004). Adolescents who struggle with word identification. In T. L. Jetton & J. A. Dole (Eds.), *Adolescent literacy research and practice* (pp. 119–134). New York: The Guilford Press.

DuFour, R., Eaker, R., & DuFour, R. (Eds.). (2005). *On common ground: The power of professional learning communities.* Bloomington, IN: National Educational Service.

Elmore, R. F. (2000). *Building a new structure for school leadership.* Washington, DC: Albert Shanker Institute.

Elmore, R. F. (2002). *Bridging the gap between standards and achievement.* Washington, DC: Albert Shanker Institute.

Elmore, R. F. (2004). *School reform from the inside out: Policy, practice, and performance.* Cambridge, MA: Harvard Education Press.

Elmore, R. F., Peterson, P. L., & McCarthey, S. J. (1996). *Restructuring in the classroom: Teaching, learning & school organization.* San Francisco: Jossey-Bass.

Fullan, M. (2001). *The new meaning of educational change.* New York: Teachers College Press.

Fullan, M. (2003). *Change forces with a vengeance.* New York: RoutledgeFalmer.

Fullan, M. (2005). *Leadership and sustainability: System thinkers in action.* Thousand Oaks, CA: Corwin Press.

Furman, S. H., & Elmore, R. F. (Eds.). (2004). *Redesigning accountability systems for education.* New York: Teachers College Press.

Garmston, R., & Wellman, B. (1999). *The adaptive school: A sourcebook for developing collaborative groups.* Norwood, MA: Christopher-Gordon.

Gladwell, M. (2000). *The tipping point: How little things can make a big difference.* Boston: Little, Brown and Company.

Granzin, A. (2006). *Traumatized learning: The emotional consequences of protracted reading difficulties.* Interview by David Boulton for Children of the Code. Retrieved November 19, 2006, from http://www.childrenofthecode.org/interviews/granzin.htm

Greene, J. F. (1998, Spring/Summer). Another chance: Help for older students with limited literacy. *American Educator, 22,* 1–2.

Greene, J. P., & Winters, M. A. (2005). *Public high school graduation and college readiness rates: 1991–2002.* New York: Manhattan Institute for Policy Research.

Hill, P. T., & Celio, M. B. (1998). *Fixing urban schools.* Washington, DC: The Brookings Institution.

Jetton, T. L., & Dole, J. A. (Eds.). (2004). *Adolescent literacy research and practice.* New York: The Guilford Press.

Kame'enui, E. J. (2004). *Differentiated curricula and assessment in reading instruction.* Interview by David Boulton for Children of the Code. Retrieved November 19, 2006, from http://www.childrenofthecode.org/interviews/kameenui.htm

Kame'enui, E. J., & Simmons, D. C. (1999). *Reading/Language Arts framework for California public schools.* Sacramento, CA: California Department of Education.

Kamil, M. L. (2003). *Adolescents and literacy: Reading for the 21st century.* Washington, DC: Alliance for Excellent Education. Retrieved November 19, 2006, from http://www.all4ed.org/publications/AdolescentsAndLiteracy.pdf

Lein, L., Johnson, J. F., Jr., Ragland, M. (1997, February). *Successful Texas schoolwide programs: Research study results.* Austin: University of Texas, Charles A. Dana Center.

Lyon, R. G. (2006). *The federal role in education.* Interview by Nancy Salvato for Education News. Retrieved November 19, 2006, from http://www.ednews.org

Marzano, R. J., Waters, T., & McNulty, B. A. (2005). *School leadership that works: From research to results.* Aurora, CO: Mid-continent Research for Education and Learning.

McCardle, P., & Chhabra, V. (Eds.). (2004). *The voice of evidence in reading research.* Baltimore: Paul H. Brookes.

McEwan, E. K. (2001). *Raising reading achievement in middle and high Schools: 5 simple-to-follow strategies for principals.* Thousand Oaks, CA: Corwin Press.

Moats, L. C. (2001). When older kids can't read. *Educational Leadership, 58*(6), 36–40.

National Institute of Child Health & Human Development (NICHD). (2000). *Report of the National Reading Panel, Teaching Children to Read: An evidence-based assessment of the scientific research literature on reading and its implications for reading instruction* (NIH Publication No. 00-4769). Washington, DC: Author.

Perie, M., Grigg, W. S., & Donahue, P. L. (2005). *The nation's report card: Reading 2005* (NCES Publication No. 2006-451). U.S. Department of Education, National Center for Education Statistics. Washington, DC: U.S. Government Printing Office.

Pressley, M. (2001, September). *Comprehension instruction: What makes sense now, what might make sense soon.* Retrieved November 19, 2006, from http://www.readingonline.org/articles/handbook/pressley/index.html

Shaywitz, S. (2003). *Overcoming dyslexia.* New York: Alfred A. Knopf.

Snow-Renner, R., & Lauer, P. A. (2005). *McREL Insights: Professional development analysis.* Denver, CO: Mid-continent Research for Education and Learning.

Stanovich, K. E. (2000). *Progress in understanding reading: Scientific foundations and new frontiers.* New York: The Guilford Press.

Torgensen, J. K. (2004). Lessons learned from research on intervention for students who have difficulty learning to read. In P. McCardle & V. Chhabra (Eds.), *The voice of evidence in reading research* (pp. 355–382). Baltimore: Paul H. Brookes.

Tuley, A. C. (1998). *Never too late to read: Language skills for the adolescent with dyslexia.* Timonium, MD: York Press.

Underwood, T., & Pearson, P. D. (2004). Teaching struggling adolescent readers to comprehend what they read. In T. L. Jetton & J. A. Dole (Eds.), *Adolescent literacy research and practice* (pp. 135–161). New York: The Guilford Press.

Zmuda, A., Kuklis, R., & Kline, E. (2004). *Transforming schools: Creating a culture of continuous improvement.* Alexandria, CA: Association of Curriculum and Development.